P9-BIW-274

LANGUAGE, LEARNING, AND COGNITIVE PROCESSES

Basic Concepts in Educational Psychology Series
Larry R. Goulet, University of Illinois, Series Editor

LANGUAGE, LEARNING, AND COGNITIVE PROCESSES

FRANCIS J. DI VESTA
The Pennsylvania State University

BROOKS/COLE PUBLISHING COMPANY
MONTEREY, CALIFORNIA
A Division of Wadsworth Publishing Company, Inc.

© 1974 by Wadsworth Publishing Company, Inc., Belmont, California 94002. All rights reserved. No part of this book may be reproduced, stored in a retrieval system, or transcribed, in any form or by any means—electronic, mechanical, photocopying, recording, or otherwise—without the prior written permission of the publisher: Brooks/Cole Publishing Company, Monterey, California 93940, a division of Wadsworth Publishing Company, Inc.

ISBN: 0–8185–0125–1
L. C. Catalog Card No.: 74–77467
Printed in the United States of America
10 9 8 7 6 5 4 3 2

Manuscript Editor: Mara Robezgruntnieks-Niels
Production Editor: Meredith Mullins
Interior & Cover Design: Linda Marcetti
Illustrations: Creative Repro, Monterey, California
Typesetting: Dharma Press, Emeryville, California
Printing & Binding: Colonial Press, Clinton, Massachusetts

SERIES FOREWORD

The present time is an exciting period in the history of education. We are reconceptualizing the nature of formal settings in which teaching and learning take place. In addition, we are developing alternative models for teaching and learning. We have rediscovered the importance of the home, parents, and peers in the educational process. And we are experiencing rapid change and continual advances in the technology of teaching and in the definition of the goals, objectives, and products of education.

The broad concern with the process of education has created new audiences for education-related courses, a demand for new course offerings, and the need for increased flexibility in the format for courses. Furthermore, colleges and schools of education are initiating new courses and curricula that appeal to the broad range of undergraduates and that focus squarely on current and relevant social and educational issues.

The Basic Concepts in Educational Psychology series is designed to provide flexibility for both the instructor and the student. The scope of the series is broad, yet each volume in the series is self-contained and may be used as either a primary or a supplementary text. In addition, the topics for the volumes in the series have been carefully chosen so that several books in the series may be adopted for use in introductory courses or in courses with a more specialized focus. Furthermore, each of the volumes is suitable for use in classes operating on the semester or quarter system, or for modular, in-service training, or workshop modes of instruction.

Larry R. Goulet

PREFACE

During the past decade, new developments in the study of language have paralleled a revitalization of interest in the learner as a processor of information. As a result, the study of cognitive processes has flourished beyond any expectations of the 1950s and early 1960s and has revealed that, to learn, the learner draws on his past experiences as much as he relies on current experiences; past and current information contribute to learning as the learner actively transforms, organizes, stores, and uses this information. These developments are important to those who are involved in modifying behavior—especially teachers and prospective teachers—since such developments provide the foundations for making decisions about specific instructional techniques and general curricular matters. Although this book was written for the student taking an undergraduate course in educational psychology, it will also interest students in the related fields of psychology, school psychology, and education of exceptional children.

At any grade level, some aspect of language dominates other aspects of language; the dominant aspect influences the way children process the information they receive, and therefore it determines the kind of instruction that will be most effective at each grade level. Accordingly, this book defines the concept of language; it examines what pupils do when they learn, recall, and transfer information; and it explains how cognitive and language processes differ among various maturational levels and among experiential settings.

Part One is a survey of the ways language can be viewed. In Chapter One, four models by which language can be studied are reviewed, together with the merits and disadvantages of each model. Chapter Two describes the elements of language—the alphabet, phonemes, morphemes, syntax, and semantics—and the way they affect behavior.

Part Two deals with the general development of language and cognition. In Chapter Three, cognitive development is described from the vantage point of Piaget's theory and in terms of its influence on intellectual and language ability. This chapter concludes with a discussion of the competence/performance distinction. The stages of language development are summarized in Chapter Four, which emphasizes grammatical and semantic factors that account for increases in complexity of language use. The concept of language universals is used to explain the relative consistency in the emergence of stages of language development.

Part Three places language in the contexts of information processing and comprehension. Chapter Five deals with the factors affecting concept formation and acquisition, the role of language in mediating the formation of categories, and the communication of affective meaning. Chapter Six explains the way language can be used to relate new material to the learner's knowledge structures; context, feature analysis, grammar, and semantic rules are shown to be tools for extracting meaning. Chapter Seven describes the contemporary views of memory and retrieval. This chapter emphasizes reconstruction processes in retrieval and distinguishes between tacit and explicit knowledge and episodic and semantic memory.

Part Four provides two specific examples of learning situations directly related to processing textual materials or connected discourse. Chapter Eight discusses what is involved in teaching reading and the differences between beginning and fluent readers. Chapter Nine is on increasing readers' comprehension of textual materials by using adjunct questions, context, behavioral objectives, advance organizers, and content hierarchies.

Part Five puts language into some of its social contexts. Chapter Ten shows how language is related to status, prestige, and power. The arguments and evidence on both sides of the deficit-difference issue are discussed, along with the social meanings of language differences and the implications of language differences for teaching. Chapter Eleven treats learning another language—either in the form of bilingualism or of a second language. It shows what consequences knowing and using two languages has on one's loyalty and on power relationships. Some programs for teaching bilingual children and for teaching a second language are presented.

Each topic in this book is related to educational theory and is presented with its linguistic basis. Terms currently used in the field are defined and discussed. Occasionally, contrasting viewpoints on selected issues are presented.

I am indebted to the many colleagues and students who read preliminary drafts of the manuscript and made helpful comments and criticisms, particularly to Charles N. Cofer, James E. Martin, and Ann Browning at The Pennsylvania State University, Paul R. Ammon at the University of California, Berkeley, Jerry L. Gray at the University of Iowa, and Larry Goulet at the University of Illinois. I have been influenced by the imaginative current works of Gordon Bower, John Carroll, Noam Chomsky, James J. Jenkins, William Labov, Endel Tulving, and many others who have made exciting contributions to the development of the study of language and cognitive psychology.

Francis J. Di Vesta

CONTENTS

UNDERSTANDING LANGUAGE

CHAPTER
ONE
FOUR MODELS
OF LANGUAGE

Acquiring language in the normal course of development is unique to humans. This achievement begins with the initial grunts, groans, cries, and gasps of the newborn infant, which are transformed into the use of single words, then into two-word utterances, and eventually into well-formed sentences. The skillful manipulation of words by statesmen, poets, and authors entrances millions, their influence often lasting for centuries. We memorize and treasure favorite sayings or poems, and the importance we attach to language is shown in our debates on the meaning and importance of words—for example, the disagreements in the late 1960s on what constitutes an obscene word or phrase, or the time and energy we devote to interpreting a sentence in a trial or in communications between nations.

The mysteries and powers of language have enchanted man for centuries. One of the first language experiments was conducted by the Egyptian king Psammetichus I about 600 BC to determine which of the two races, Egyptian or Phrygian, was the original race of man (see de Selincourt, 1964). He obtained two infants of average parentage as subjects and assigned them to a shepherd who served as the experimenter. The children were to be fed goats' milk and be adequately cared for in all ways except that no word was to be spoken in their presence. The first real word to emerge from the babbling of these infants was hypothesized to indicate the priority of the races. When the children were about 2 years old, the shepherd reported that the word *becos* was constantly repeated. After satisfying himself that this was a reliable observation, Psammetichus made further inquiries and found that this word was Phrygian for *bread*. Accordingly, he concluded that the Phrygians were the original race.

Psammetichus' experiment was not without its weaknesses, but it does show an early concern with the role of language in people's lives. The study of language continues to challenge us today.

THE STUDY OF LANGUAGE

Until the 1960s, the investigation of language was considered the sole domain of the linguists. Their analyses consisted of the structural analysis of distinctive sounds in the language (called *phonemes*), the sequence of connected sounds (called *morphemes*), and the organization of words into phrases and sentences (called *syntax*). Scientists in other disciplines took little interest in such matters. Early experimental psychologists admitted that language helped stabilize experiences for storage and retrieval, and they concerned themselves with how often words recurred, as reflected in word counts, and with the associative value of words, as reflected in the number of associations with nonsense syllables and common words.

Early investigators of verbal phenomena had a naive understanding of the characteristics of the language they wanted to explain. Today we realize that the complexity of language encompasses its grammar, semantics, biological bases, acquisition, development, influence on behavior, and social context; we now realize that the study of language requires the harmonious interdisciplinary efforts of the biologist, linguist, psychologist, sociologist, and anthropologist.

How a scientist views language depends on his objectives, which are in turn inevitably related to his discipline. Lenneberg (1969) has examined the evidence for innate biological capacities in the acquisition of language. Gardner and Gardner (1971) and Premack (1971) have taught chimpanzees to acquire vocabulary, simple sentences, and logical relationships through contrived communication devices. Others, such as Bloom (1970), Brown (1973a, 1973b), and McNeill (1971), have studied the acquisition of one's first language.

Because of the interrelations among these concerns, at least two new fields of investigation have emerged in an attempt to achieve an interdisciplinary view of language as a system: *psycholinguistics* combines psychology and linguistics into one field, and *sociolinguistics* combines sociology and linguistics into one field. This book is based largely on research from these two fields and from psychology.

Dember and Jenkins (1970) present four models that clarify the different levels from which an investigator might approach the *psychological* analysis of language. The following discussion of each model shows the conclusions that might result from each level.

Model I: Language as words
Model II: Language as strings of words or word classes

Model III: Language as utterances
Model IV: Language as a structural system*

LANGUAGE AS WORDS

Model I emphasizes words in isolation. Words can be counted, their frequency noted, and their frequency of association with other words identified. One can count the number of times a word is used by age groups, grade groups, school readers, magazines, or newspapers. Words can be rated on scales for degree of familiarity, imagery, pronounceability, or concreteness. The meanings of isolated words can be identified by dictionary definitions or by the number of different associations subjects give as responses in a free-association test.

Studies of these properties of words show that they are important in learning and transfer: high-frequency words, concrete or high-imagery words, and easily pronounced words are learned more readily than low-frequency words, low-imagery words, or difficult-to-pronounce words. These variables are so important that all studies of verbal learning manipulate them to examine their effects or to control for their effects.

LANGUAGE AS STRINGS OF WORDS
OR WORD CLASSES

Model II views language as strings of words. It goes beyond model I by stating that language uses words in certain non-arbitrary sequences; some words are more likely than others to be connected in a sentence or an association. The "cloze technique" (Taylor, 1953), used to determine the readability of a passage, is based on this idea. In this procedure, words are deleted from a passage and the reader is asked to fill in the omitted word, as in the following sentences:

A _____ is an alkaloid isomeric.
The polite old gentleman always _____ his hat when he met a _____.
Do you want to know what the wolf did to the _____?
He _____ the sheep.

Some of the missing words are easier to identify than others. The likelihood of identifying the correct word depends on, first, the properties of single words—that is, how familiar and frequently used it is. Second, identification

* Based on Chapter 12 of *General Psychology: Modeling Behavior and Experience*, by W. N. Dember & J. J. Jenkins. Copyright ©1970 by Prentice-Hall, Inc. Used by permission.

depends on the context—that is, the preceding and following words serve as a cue—which shows that language is a string of words.

Some sequences have higher frequency in the language than others. Americans will fill in the following sentences in a very consistent, although not necessarily unanimous, way:

> The boy hit the _____ (ball, girl).
> Communism and _____ (socialism) contrast sharply with democracy.

The sequence of words is also studied through word associations. The usual procedure is to present one word as a stimulus, to which the subject responds with the first word that comes to mind. Responses to the word *mother* might include *father, family, daughter,* or *woman.* Responses to the word *chair* might include *table, sit,* or *furniture.* By looking at responses to a number of different words, other correspondences can be noted. The word *round* might be associated with *compass, square, apple,* and *collar.* Interestingly, none of these four words are usually associated with each other.

Sometimes the associations are of the same form class (*mother, father*), and sometimes they are of different form classes (*deep, hole*). Children tend to use different form classes (called *syntagmatic* associations) while adults use the same form class (called *paradigmatic* associations) (Ervin, 1961). Paradigmatic associations are used more often with familiar than with less familiar words (Jenkins & Palermo, 1964). Membership in a conceptual category (for example, *cow, fox,* and *elephant* are all animals) may also be bases for word associations.

Word associations are influential in learning. Responses learned to a novel stimulus such as LVM (stimulus, LVM; response, *chair*) will transfer to facilitate other learning in which the new response is a common associate of the first response (stimulus, LVM; response, *table*). That is, it will be much easier to learn LVM → *table* if the person first learned LVM→ *chair* than if he had learned LVM → *king.* Word associations also convey meaning; for example, to identify a new insect, we might say, "It is like a butterfly." In addition, associations can link such apparently unrelated words as *flower* and *pain* if we present a sequence like *flower, rose, thorn, pain. Rose* might be an associate of *flower, thorn* of *rose,* and *pain* of *thorn.* Although *flower* does not by itself typically elicit *pain* as an associate, the association can be learned more readily if intermediate links are provided than if they are not.

We make similar associations in everyday problem solving. For example, someone needs a screwdriver but none is available. Through associative processes, he reasons that a screwdriver has a thin edge, that coins have thin edges, and that therefore a coin can be substituted for a screwdriver; coins are not typical associates of screwdrivers unless they are linked by the quality of having a thin edge. Another example: learners who will need to make a pendulum to solve a problem—when given a preview of this concept by being asked, first, to learn words such as *swing*—perform the problem better than do those who learn words unrelated to the functions of a pendulum. This instructional technique is sometimes called *priming* (Cofer, 1957).

Word associations influence the way words are retrieved or recalled (Seibel, 1965, 1966). When a list of several words and their associates is presented singly and in random order, subjects group them as pairs during recall. The learner imposes this grouping on the list, since the word and its associate were presented initially in widely separated positions. When words can be associated by conceptual categories, they will be recalled in clusters even though they were presented in a different order.

Associations are psychologically meaningful. Knowing that sequences of words have orderly properties can serve practical purposes. Fluent readers (and good listeners) grasp the meaning of sentences quickly because certain words in a sentence can be anticipated, even skipped, when they have high probabilities of occurrence in given contexts. Word associations facilitate learning through generalization (or transfer), reasoning through mediational links, problem solving by priming associations, and remembering (or retrieval of information).

LANGUAGE AS UTTERANCES

Model III describes language as utterances. It is based on B. F. Skinner's work (1957), in which language is considered an aspect of behavior in general. Skinner implies that language consists of functional units whose importance can be strengthened or weakened by the application of rewards.

Skinner's analysis views verbal behavior as a way of controlling the environment, on the one hand, and of classifying environmental events, on the other. These are called the *mand* and *tact* functions, respectively. Mands, derived from de*mands* and com*mands*, require action from the listener—that is, the speaker attempts to control the behavior of others for his benefit. Mands permit the listener to infer something about the state of the speaker regardless of external circumstances. Typical mands are "Get me the books"; "Put those chairs here"; "Throw the ball to me"; or "Come here." Tacts, meaning that words provide con*tact* with the world, tell the listener what the speaker has to say about the world. Tacts permit inferences about external circumstances exclusive of the state of the speaker. Characteristically, they involve naming, classification, reference, or other descriptions of some aspect of the world. They may take the form of "This object is a ball"; "Arachnids do not belong to the same class as insects"; or "Daddy is coming home." Since tacts describe some stimulus property, they can be the bases of concepts.

Other classes of verbal behavior underlie the formation of mand and tact forms. *Echoic verbal behaviors* occur in imitating language patterns used by others. *Textual verbal behaviors* are involved in acquisition from reading. *Intraverbal behaviors* involve the formation of associations and sequences of words that are the building blocks for more elaborate constructions. *Autoclitic verbal behaviors* are used to tell the listener something—"I declare [this to be the truth]"; to tell the listener about the strength of the speakers' statements—"I can't say [that I am right]"; to tell the listener about the relations between the verbal responses of speaker and listener—"I agree [with you]"; or to tell the listener about the emotional or motivational state of the speaker—"I am happy to say [that you will get a raise in salary]."

The acquisition of these classes of verbal behavior occurs in the context of other environmental events and behaviors: a given set of circumstances (discriminated stimulus) motivates the individual to give a certain response (echoing, demanding, or naming). In this context, the response is called an *operant* since it functions to operate on the environment. If the response is appropriate, it is reinforced by its success. For example, in the development of a mand, the child might be thirsty (motive). An adult who can potentially administer the reinforcer (provide milk) is present. The adult is a discriminated stimulus, and his presence is the occasion on which a demand will be functionally useful. The child then responds by making the demand—that is, saying "milk." The milk he receives reinforces him.

The operant-conditioning framework directs our attention to characteristic environments in which language is learned. Learning a language always involves a speaker and a listener interdependently; thus, language is useful to man as one way to adjust to the world around him.

Skinner's complete analysis (1957) points to a larger system than learning isolated words or word sequences. Skinner analyzed classes of verbal behavior and the conditions for modifying them as one facet of all behavior. This analysis has been questioned on a number of grounds (Chomsky, 1959), including its being only an analogy to experiments on the performance of subhuman organisms. As a consequence, it may have only limited application to investigations of language behavior.

A major criticism of the operant-conditioning approach is that its emphasis on external events of stimulus control, operants (responses), and reinforcements is used exclusively to explain behavior (Chomsky, 1959). This approach ignores the speaker's contribution of processing the language information he receives, of forming hypotheses about language from this information, and of generalizing these hypotheses in the form of rules to generate new sentences. Skinner's approach ignores what appear to be innate tendencies or abilities that lead to the acquisition of similar grammars of amazing complexity by all children of all languages.

LANGUAGE AS A STRUCTURAL SYSTEM

Chomsky's works (1957, 1959, 1965) have led to a major reorientation in psychological research that is reflected in model IV, which views language as a structural system; this model is based on language usage being more than the acquisition of a finite set of sentences that can be used when the speaker needs one of them. In no language is the set of all sentences exactly the same whether heard, spoken, or written. Theoretically, no set of sentences will represent a given language since an infinite number of grammatically correct sentences can be generated. Consequently, one does not appear to learn language by building from words to sequences to sentences. Nor does one appear to learn a set of exemplary sentences, store them away, and use them later to measure the adequacy of any new sentence whether heard, spoken, or read.

What is the alternative? According to model IV, language acquisition and use involve cognitive processes—mainly learning interlocking sets of rules that govern the production (as opposed to the reproduction) of sentences. These rules are used at all levels of language production: the production of unique sounds (phonemes), the combinations of sound into words (morphemes), the linking of words into phrases, and the linking of phrases into sentences. When one puts a meaning into the form of a spoken sentence, he behaves as though he uses these rules.

Language can be described linguistically as a set of rules for placing words into noun phrases, main verbs, auxiliaries, and predicate phrases. There are rules—called *productive rules*—for changing an active sentence into a passive sentence or for changing positive sentences into negative sentences. There are rules for using a word as a noun ("I bought a *permit* for building a house") or as a verb ("*Permit* me to explain my point"). Which rules we use depend on the meaning we want to convey and how we want to express that meaning. This illustrates the supposition that ". . . language is 'computed' rather than 'stored' and that this is what accounts for our tremendous capacity to utter novel but appropriate sentences and to understand new sentences when we hear them" (Dember & Jenkins, 1970, p. 463).

The rules are apparently learned and used intuitively—that is, people may not know or be able to define the rules. To illustrate, examine the four sentences that follow.

John picked up the ball.
John picked the ball up.
John picked up it.
John picked it up.

All readers can identify the third sentence as grammatically incorrect, yet few can identify the rules they used to make their decision. The linguist's task is to identify the rules. The psychologist's task is to determine whether these rules actually influence behavior.

CHAPTER TWO

LANGUAGE STRUCTURES

Linguists describe the characteristics of the language system in terms of phonemes, morphemes, and syntax. Chapter Two will examine how these elements reflect behavior and the way learners process and use their knowledge of the language. This chapter begins with the smallest unit of speech, the phoneme; next, it discusses the larger units, morphemes and phrases; it concludes with the structure of language as a system of rules.

ELEMENTS OF LANGUAGE

THE ALPHABET

Pictograms. The alphabet emerged in a number of stages (Huey, 1908), originating in picture writing or *pictograms* that portrayed objects and events directly. These one-to-one relationships between writing and experience became conventionalized as *ideographs* to include feelings: for example, conflict became represented by two arrows separated by a bar, → | ←, rather than two groups of men facing each other; a clasped hand was used to indicate peace. Ideographs were cumbersome when used to express complex events, so *determinants* were sometimes added to help resolve possible ambiguities; for example, an ear (a determinant) between two doors is more readily interpreted as "listen" than the two doors alone.

Phonograms. Picture-writing became cumbersome. Too many symbols were required to represent all ideas that might be communicated. The major transition in developing the alphabet was the gradual invention of the *phonogram*, a pictorial sign to represent sounds. For example, a cask (called a *tun*) with a thistle (*burr*) on it could be used as a symbol for the proper name "Burton," and a picture of a pear could be used for *pare* and *pair*. This kind of symbolization is kept alive today in many children's books and is known as *rebus-writing*.

Syllabaries.   The syllabaries of the Chinese and Japanese show a direct relationship between signs and sounds, although syllabaries occur in other languages as well. The Chinese have hundreds of phonetic signs (signs that represent sounds) and keys (signs for expressions and intonations) that can be combined to produce tens of thousands of words. Most of these have to be learned in more or less rote fashion. Interestingly, the Chinese and Japanese have never developed an alphabet, although they are currently taking steps to do so.

Acrology.   The syllabary was accompanied by the *acrology*—picture-symbols that represent the initial sounds of words. In today's usage, this would be comparable to using the phrase "Apple is for A" or "Boy is for B" and so on for all distinguishable sounds. The easiest-to-reproduce part of the picture was eventually abstracted to substitute for the whole and thereby simplified writing. For example, the letter *m* may have originated in the Egyptian hieroglyphic for owl, or *mulak*, in which the top part of the owl's head represented the letter *m* and came to substitute for the whole picture.

The alphabet.   The last stage in the development of the alphabet as we know it can probably be traced to the Greeks and Romans. In this phase, the abstracted features of pictures were regularly used to represent sounds. Eventually, a few basic sounds (phonemes) were identified; they could be combined in many ways to form all the words in the language. This remarkable insight restricted the number of necessary letters in the alphabet and has contributed considerably to its efficiency. Despite the vagaries of rules for combining letters to form letter-sound correspondences, the alphabet is still the best means available for communication by writing. Attempts to reform the alphabet, even for teaching reading, have never met with more than dampened enthusiasm.

PHONEMES

The 26 letters (graphemes) of the alphabet might reasonably be expected to have 26 corresponding basic sounds in speech, one letter for each distinguishable speech sound. However, the English language has about 46 basic sounds, although this number varies among all languages from as few as 15 to as many as 85 basic sounds. Some letters do have distinctive sounds, but sometimes letters must be combined to represent unique sounds or two or more letters may have the same sound.

Theoretically, a limitless number of sound differentiations (phones) produced by a speaker could be identified by a highly sensitive electronic instrument. The spoken /k/* in *caught* and *kin*, or the /d/ in *dim* and *doom* can be distinguished by such an apparatus, as can minor differences in the way any basic sound is actually formed by the same speaker in different words or contexts or when using different intonations or dialects. Despite the many measurable distinctions, sounds are not perceived by the speaker/listener to have so many differences. Instead, the listener imposes regularity on this multiplicity of sounds by grouping similar sounds into one of the 46 categories. Within a category, all of the sounds are functionally equivalent, acting as a single signaling unit called a *phoneme*.

Phoneme production. Although the slightly different sounds that are considered one phoneme are, for practical purposes, nearly indistinguishable from one another, each phoneme is different from other phonemes in one or more ways—for example, the /r/ in *rill* is different from the /g/ in *rouge*. For consonants, these differences include characteristics of voice (either vibrating the vocal cords or not—for example, /b/ in *boy* and /p/ in *pin*); and friction (producing in the air passage either a narrow slit opening—for example, /f/ in *fill*—or a narrow grooved opening—for example, /z/ in *zeal*). The presence or absence of any of these characteristics can be combined with other characteristics to form other phonemes, such as voiced stops (for example, /b/ in *bill*). The linguist makes many more differentiations, but these examples show that sound characteristics correspond to the way the sound is produced.

Phonemes are not used mechanically either in speaking or listening. Even at this most basic level of the language system, sounds are processed by both the transmitter (speaker) and the receiver (listener). Classes of sounds are constructed by principles analogous to those involved in concept formation and concept identification. From this point of view, a phoneme is considered a concept that consists of a class of sounds with common features (Jakobson, 1968). Features are abstracted from a variety of instances and all instances with those features are grouped together as a class. Rules for combining different features are acquired in the process.

Phonemes and behavior. Some data suggest that the distinctive contrasts among phonemic classes may have some bearing on behavior. The most direct parallel is in concept learning. The learner does seem to distinguish the contrasts and to disregard the irrelevant features of sound structures when learning a phoneme class (Fries, 1964, pp. 35–92, 222–232). When two phonemes differ on several distinctive features they can be separated

---

* For convenience, phonemes will be designated by the linguistic convention of a letter enclosed in two slash marks / /.

more easily, identified without confusion, and learned more easily than can phonemes with fewer contrasting features (Greenberg & Jenkins, 1964; Jenkins, Foss, & Greenberg, 1968). Even 1-month-old infants seem to be able to discriminate among phonemic features that approximate differences among major phoneme classes. However, children at this age cannot discriminate among the more subtle sound differences within categories (Anisfeld & Gordon, 1968). The ability to produce phonemic patterns begins at about 1 year of age and is followed by increasing ability to combine phonemes into sequences to form words. The greatest difficulty in this achievement is acquiring rules for combining consonants into clusters—an achievement that may not be reached until the child is 8 years old (Templin, 1957).

Other evidence indicates that children respond to phonemic categories. When required to distinguish among possible plural alternatives for artificial words, elementary school children tend to choose the plural form most similar to the /s/ or /z/ form commonly used to form plurals in English (Messer, 1967). Similarly, when choosing between two artificial monosyllabic words, 3-year-old children tend to choose the word that follows the rules of English. The child's final language acquisition consists of stress within words (such as the differences between pictograph and pictography, produce and production), and the use of intonations in forming sentences (such as the rising intonation at the end of questions). The last accomplishment is remarkable because although the phonemes the child hears are always accompanied by rising and falling intonations (*prosodic features*) and the intonations remain the same for an individual speaker, the intonations vary considerably among speakers. Yet the listener is not confused by these differences, which implies that the listener responds to patterns of sounds—as he does to a melody even though it may change from one key to another—rather than to the absolute characteristics of the sounds.

Although some evidence supports the idea that phonemes are perceived by the listener, other evidence questions this idea and even the usefulness of the concept of the phoneme (Wickelgren, 1969). Savin and Bever (1970), for example, indicate that phoneme identification is not based on articulatory movements or acoustic stimuli alone but instead depends on the context in which it occurs—that is, on the syllable. Accordingly, the syllable is recognized first, followed by recognition of the phoneme. Anything that facilitates recognition of the syllable facilitates detection of the phoneme. It is the syllable that is perceived by the listener, not the phoneme. Nevertheless, Savin and Bever (1970) have noted that subjects did seem to understand what to look for when instructed to identify specific phonemes. Furthermore, these investigators suggest that such phenomena as the emergence of the alphabet, certain forms of rhymes and alliteration, and spoonerisms support the idea that phonemes are perceived, so they are in favor of retaining the phoneme as a useful tool in understanding language.

MORPHEMES

Phonemes are combined into larger units called *morphemes,* the smallest meaningful spoken unit. Although somewhat synonymous with *word,* linguists prefer to define *morpheme* more precisely. They say a morpheme is a language unit that cannot be broken down further without losing or altering its meaning (Gleason, 1960). Consider the words *Georgia, boy,* and *mother.* They are single morphemes since they cannot be segmented without altering their meanings. On the other hand, *boys* and *goes* can be broken down into two morphemes and still retain a meaning close to the original meaning: *boys* consists of /boy/ and /z/, and *goes* of /go/ and /z/. To illustrate this distinction more clearly, compare *goes* (/go/ + /z/) with *rose,* which must be kept a single unit (/rowz/) to retain its meaning. However, when *rose* is changed to its plural form, *roses,* it consists of two morphemes (/rowz/ + /iz/).

A single morpheme may consist of one syllable (*boy*) or several syllables (*Georgia*). A morpheme can change one form of a word into another form, as when /er/ is added to *box* to form *boxer*; however, when the presence of a morpheme does not change the form of the word—for example, as with /er/ in *mother*—it is not a morpheme. Some morphemes stand by themselves, as *boy* or *book* do, in which case they are *free morphemes.* Words can be constructed by combining free morphemes—for example, *bookshelf* and *doorstop.* Other kinds of morphemes must be used with another morpheme, as the /z/ must be used to form plurals, in which case they are called *bound morphemes.* Still other morphemes are alike in all situations, as is the /ing/ in *closing, turning,* and *running.*

Morpheme development.   Many rules for forming morphemes have been described by linguists. Everyone who speaks a language is competent in using these rules, although probably no one gives much thought to them in speaking. These rules are not learned by imitative processes alone, as we see when the child misuses language: when he says "I *bringed* my tricycle home," "I *camed* from the store," or "Those are my *footses,*" he is unlikely to be imitating others, certainly not adults. Such utterances help us understand how the child's mind functions. In this case, we infer that the child has learned a rule for forming plurals or verb inflections. Though it may be incorrect by adult standards of speech, it is consistent in children's speech.

There is an important distinction between imitation and learning a rule. If the child's speech were correct by adult standards, we could not be certain whether the child was parroting what he had heard or had determined a rule. By noting his distortion of the language, we see that the child is somehow processing information into a generalizable rule. At this stage (3 or 4 years old), the child overgeneralizes.

Glinging. In a much cited series of studies, Berko (1958) investigated the morphological rules of verb inflection and noun pluralization used by children. Her procedure was to show groups of younger and older children a set of caricatures of small animals, birds, or people. First, a card would be presented to the child followed by a comment such as, "This is a *wug.*" Then another card with the same creature would be shown alongside the first card. The experimenter then would say, "Now there is another one. There are two of them." The subsequent statement contained a blank. It required the child to respond by saying the plural of *wug*: "There are two _____." Berko also showed pictures of a man swinging a pail over his head. Here she used such statements as "This is a person who knows how to *gling.* He *glings* every day. Today he *glings.* Yesterday he _____."

Berko's experiments showed increasing precision in the use of standard rules with age. About 75 percent of preschool children and 99 percent of the first-graders responded with the correct plural of such words as *wug* (*wugs*) even though they had never heard it before. All the young children added the regular form of /ed/ to *gling* to form the past tense (*glinged*). However, most of the older group, probably because of their wider experience with irregular verbs, made the past tense of *gling* into *glang* or *glung.* About half of Berko's 28 items successfully differentiated the younger from the older group. Young children made errors in forming plurals even when the correct form was stated explicitly by the experimenter: "Here is a *goose.* Here are two geese. There are two _____." Most of the children used *gooses* to fill in the blank. These findings show how imitation tendencies are overpowered by the overgeneralized rule even when children are offered the correct answer.

Chomsky says, "It is by no means obvious that the child of 6 has mastered a phonological system in full—he may not yet have been presented with all the evidence that determines the general structure of the English sound pattern" (Chomsky, 1964, p.7). The formal evidence regarding the acquisition of the sound system clearly corresponds to the anecdotal evidence. It indicates that the child does have much to learn even after age 5, although he has already learned a great deal; he has learned some highly intricate rules, he has acquired the rudimentary content of the structure of his language, he can use these rules in a generative system—that is, he can derive new combinations based on those expressions already learned—that provides for tremendous flexibility in expression and content.

SYNTACTICAL STRUCTURES

The rules for combining morphemes (words) into grammatically proper sentences or strings—that is, into well-formed sentences—are called syntax, which is based on linguists' analyses of sentence formation. The psychologist's task is to evaluate the soundness of the assumed structure by such methods as observing its behavioral correlates or studying developmental trends. The goal of syntactical description is to identify the relations among words in, and as parts of, sentences. The ultimate purpose, of course, is to understand how the meaning of sentences is conveyed by the speaker to the listener.

Many alternatives for describing rules of syntax have been proposed, but the process has proven to be much more complicated than once believed. For example, initial research on developing translation techniques via computer programming was futile. Programs were constructed to replace words in one language with their equivalents in another by simple ordering rules. This procedure failed because words in one order may convey a different meaning from the same words in another order. As Smith (1971) suggests, "a Maltese cross" does not mean the same thing as "a cross Maltese" nor does "a Venetian blind" mean the same thing as "a blind Venetian." Other more or less mechanical attempts to understand meaning as a sum total of words met with failure.

Sometimes the order of the words in a sentence may provide clues to the intended meaning of a communication. Order can be helpful when the nouns are irreversible. The construction and meaning of the sentence "The fence was hit by the boy" is clear. When the two nouns are reversed, however, the sentence typically conveys little meaning. But in a sentence such as "They are eating apples" the order of the words does not help us understand the meaning: does the sentence refer to a kind of apple or to a group of people who are eating apples? Chapter Three will show why these ambiguities occur and how they are resolved.

KNOWLEDGE UNDERLYING GRAMMATICAL USE

Grammar is based on the assumption that word meanings alone are insufficient for communicating ideas. Words must be combined into sentences if they are to communicate purposes, intentions, or expressions of feelings. The way words are combined makes a difference in their meaning. Grammar describes the rules underlying the regularities or structures of word combinations and views language as a way of forming statements so we can communicate.

Any grammar assumes that the speaker already has a lexicon (a vocabulary of the words one has of his language) and at least an implicit knowledge of grammar. For example, while you may not be able to state explicitly the specific rules for using count nouns and mass nouns in conjunction with articles, such rules as the following would be reflected in your writing and speech: count nouns represent objects whose singularity and shape can be easily identified—for example, house, tree, bean, animal, triangle. When used in sentences, they are preceded by an article, such as *a, an,* or *the.* Whether you use *a* or *an* depends on whether the subsequent word begins with a vowel (*an owl* but not *a owl*) or a consonant (*a dog* but not *an dog*). Mass nouns refer to objects without definite form that consist of many particles such as sand, water, rice, molasses. They are not preceded by the definite articles *a* or *an.* Unlike count nouns, mass nouns generally cannot be pluralized. The plural and the singular of the mass noun are the same: a grain of rice, four quarts of molasses, or four bags of sand. Specialized uses of mass nouns do exist, of course, as in "the waters raged" and "the sands of time," but in common usage mass nouns are not pluralized.

There are rules for each class of *content words* (nouns, verbs, adjectives, adverbs), which refer to specific things in the environment, and *function words* (articles, prepositions, conjunctions), which are used to express relationships. The user of the language implicitly knows these rules even though he may have had no formal instruction in them. All of us know much more about a word than just its dictionary definition. Such knowledge is the essential basis for using the grammars to be discussed next.

PHRASE-STRUCTURE GRAMMAR

Phrase-structure grammar analyzes a sentence by dividing it into its constituent parts. The rules of phrase-structure grammar are built around phrases. These phrases are further subdivided into their constituent parts. The largest components of a sentence (*S*), from this point of view, are its noun phrase (*NP*) and its verb phrase (*VP*), which correspond roughly to the subject and predicate you may have learned in secondary school. But phrase-structure grammar does more than merely describe the parts of a sentence; it provides rules for combining phrases and parts of phrases.

Rules.   Three elementary rules will illustrate the application of this grammar. They are:

1. $S \rightarrow NP + VP$
   (This means that the sentence is broken down into the noun phrase and verb phrase.)

2. $VP \rightarrow V + NP$
(This means the verb phrase can be further broken down into the verb and a noun phrase.)

3. $NP \rightarrow (Art) + ((Adv) + Adj^n) + N$
(A noun phrase may consist of a noun by itself, a noun combined with an article, or a noun with one or more adjectives or adverbs preceding it. The second set of parentheses shows that adjectives can appear by themselves or, optionally, with an adverb.)

Rule 3 allows the noun to be modified by an extensive list of adjectives or adverbial modifiers. The parentheses indicate that one is not obliged to use articles, adverbs, or adjectives since the noun may exist in the noun phrase by itself, as it would in the sentence "Bill (*NP*) ran home (*VP*)."

A language also needs real words (lexical items) that can be substituted for symbols—for example:

$Art \rightarrow$ a, an, the . . .
$Adj \rightarrow$ big, good, dirty, old, high, weak . . .
$Adv \rightarrow$ very, extremely, slightly . . .
$N \rightarrow$ dog, boy, fence, bone, ball, tree, Mary, biscuits, Bill . . .
$V \rightarrow$ hit, caught, chased, jumped, climbed . . .

Tree diagrams.   Grammatical sentences can now be constructed from these rules. By using rules 1, 2, and 3 we can construct "Bill chased Mary" (the article is not used in rule 3) and "The cat chased the dog" (the article is used in both noun phrases according to rule 3). By using the options provided in all the rules, we can construct a sentence like "The very big, old dog chased the slightly weak, little cat."

Particularly important in phrase-structure grammar is its hierarchical structure that can be graphically displayed in a tree diagram to represent the application of rules, as shown in Figure 2-1.

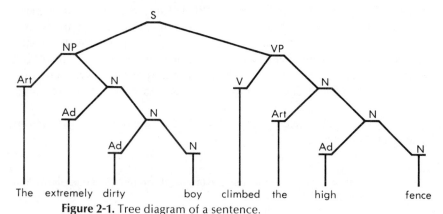

Figure 2-1. Tree diagram of a sentence.

Eating apples. Note that many other rules are needed to construct more complex sentences. The rules presented here illustrate only that sequencing rules allow an analysis of the meaning of sentences. For example, consider the ambiguity of the sentence we used earlier, "They are eating apples." By analyzing this sentence, we can see that it has two meanings, as Figure 2-2 shows.

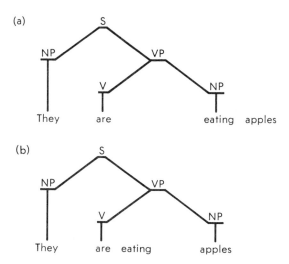

Figure 2-2. "They are eating apples."

In (a), *eating* is more closely related to the noun *apples* (as part of the predicate nominative construction) and describes a kind of apple. In (b), *eating* is related to *are* (in the single progressive verb *are eating*), thereby conveying the notion that something is being done to the apples.

Clicks and phrases. Analyses of this sort seem to correspond to cognitive processes. For example, imagine a subject listening to a tape recording of a sentence. Superimposed on this recording is a click. The subject's task is to indicate the point of click. In the first of many studies, Ladefoged (1959) found that subjects erred by several phonemes in locating where the click occurred. They moved the click one way or another to correspond with the end of a morpheme or other apparently logical break. In fact, subjects sometimes moved the click to a point that corresponded to the end of a major clause (Fodor & Bever, 1965).

In another study, Garrett, Bever, and Fodor (1966) used two versions of the beginning of a sentence while retaining the same seven words at the end of the sentence in each version. Intonations for the last seven words in each version were identical since duplicate tape recordings were used. The two versions provided different structures for the sentence such that the first set of duplicated words occurred earlier in the phrase structure of its sentence than the second set did in its sentence. (This is similar to saying "These are McIntosh apples. They are eating apples" in one experimental variation and "They are at a picnic. They are eating apples" in another variation. In both versions the last four words are the same, although the phrase structures differ.) When the click was placed over the middle of the last seven words it was perceived much later in the sentence. (In our illustration, if a click had been superimposed on the first syllable of *eating*, it would have been reported as occurring after *are* in the first version and after *eating* in the second version.)

Such findings imply that people process or reconstruct what they hear in chunks or segments. The way a sentence can be segmented provides at least one important cognitive unit in the way the sentence is processed. When we listen or read, we focus on the entire sentence or phrase, not on the individual words; we get our meaning from the longer structures. For example, it is difficult to imagine a word like *under* or *running* by itself, but when we say "The cat is under the table" or "The boy is running," imagery is much easier.

Phrase-structure grammar describes one level of sentence construction; it breaks the sentence down into its constituent parts and provides rules for ordering those parts. When using phrase-structure grammars, the rules for rewriting sentences are followed explicitly, phrase by phrase.

The drawback of phrase-structure grammar is that many rules are required to form all possible kinds of sentences. Thus, one set of rules is required to write "The boy hit the ball" and another set to write "The ball was hit by the boy" even though the two sentences obviously have similar meanings, as would whole classes of other sentences derived from them—their interrogative, passive, and imperative forms and their past, present, and future tenses. Furthermore, phrase-structure grammar fails to account for the speaker/listener's knowledge about the language—his competence. It represents the sentence directly from the grammar.

TRANSFORMATIONAL GRAMMAR

To compensate for apparent deficiencies in phrase-structure and similar grammars, Chomsky (1957) proposed transformational grammar, based on a single string of words known as a simple, active, affirmative, declarative (sometimes abbreviated as SAAD), or kernel sentence. By applying a system of rules to the kernel sentence, it could be represented in several ways: one set of rules could be used to make it a question, another to make it an imperative, and another to make it a passive statement. You could stop at the kernel sentence, presumably, if you wanted to discover the meaning of any sentence.

Base and surface structures.   Shortly after proposing this system, Chomsky (1965) revised his position (see Katz & Postal, 1964) to mean that the grammar operated on the base structure rather than on the kernel sentence. The base structure represented the meaning to be conveyed; the surface structure was the form that meaning took—whether, passive, active, stated as a question, or as any other variation. For example, these two sentences have the same base structure:

> The teacher calls Bill. (active)
> Bill is called by the teacher. (passive)

However, the surface structure of the sentences varies in the sequence of words, their length, the additional words in the second sentence, and the reversal of the two nouns although the listener/reader extracts the same meaning from both sentences. The transformational rule has been applied in each case to the nucleus (the active base in the first sentence and the passive base in the second) so that the meaning is unchanged. In other words, in both sentences, the teacher is the subject/agent and Bill is the object/recipient of the action.

Chomsky later clarified the semantic difference between such sentences as

> The teacher calls Bill.
> The teacher doesn't call Bill.

Since they have different meanings, they must also have different base structures. This fact is noted by a designation, or "trigger" that indicates the kind of transformation applied. Thus,

> The teacher calls Bill. (positive)

becomes

> The teacher does not call Bill. (negative)

The range of most transformations represented in the English language is illustrated in these sentences:

> The teacher doesn't call Bill. (negative)
> Does the teacher call Bill? (question)

Bill is not called by the teacher. (negative-passive)
Doesn't the teacher call Bill? (negative-question)
Is Bill called by the teacher? (passive-question)
Isn't Bill called by the teacher? (negative-passive question)

Did Bill prove the theorem?   The importance of the base structure is illustrated by the following sentences.

Bill proved the theorem. (active)
The theorem was proved by Bill. (passive)
The theorem proves Bill. (ungrammatical)
Bill is proved by the theorem. (ungrammatical)

The first two sentences have different surface structures but similar base structures, or meanings. Again, the base structure is represented in the surface structure by *someone* + *proves* + *something*. The last two sentences, however, are ungrammatical. Without considering semantics, one noun *could* be used interchangeably with another in the way shown. Thus, they are not ungrammatical due to placement of words but because of semantics. First, these sentences do not represent the base structure; they say, in effect, *something* + *proves* + *someone*. Second, the subject of the ungrammatical sentence violates the rule that requires the verb *to prove* to have an animate subject.

By using base structures, we can account for ambiguities in a sentence like:

John knows a taller man than Bill.

It can have two base structures:

(1) John knows a man who is taller than Bill is.
(2) John knows a man who is taller than a man whom Bill knows.

Thus, we can see that a base structure has all the information needed for both syntactic and semantic interpretation of the surface structure. The base structure can yield many surface structures, depending on which transformations are used.

MEANING, GRAMMAR, AND COMMUNICATION

Chomsky's theory has three systems of rules: semantic rules for interpreting and conveying meaning in sentences; syntactical rules for interpreting and conveying the surface structure expression of the spoken sentence; and phonological rules for pairing sounds with their corresponding meaning. Through our implicit knowledge of such rules we are intuitively able to judge whether sentences are equivalent to each other and whether they are grammatical.

Thus, meaning and grammar are related but not identical. The speaker/writer originates a meaning he wants to communicate. This is his base structure. Transformational rules are applied to the base structure to generate the surface structure of the sentence that is used in communication. This is further transformed into whatever phonological system is to be used. So, although meaning is related to grammar, grammar is not necessarily related to meaning, as the following discussion will show.* For example, the sentence, "Mommy shoe," which a child might utter, is ambiguous. Does the child want his shoe tied? Is he saying a certain shoe belongs to his mother? Does he want his shoe? When the child points to his mother's shoe, his intended meaning becomes clearer. The context provides the necessary information for an interpretation. Mothers rarely have trouble with such utterances because they do use contextual information, although the grammar, alone, is inadequate for determining the child's intended meaning.

A similar sentence is *"Like girls boys,"* in which the grammar has been disrupted. The reader can make several meanings out of it: either *girls* or *boys* can be the agent or object of *like*, or *like* may be being used in a comparative sense, as in "Like girls, boys also grow long hair." The intended meaning cannot become clear merely by making the sentence grammatical. Other contextual cues will be required.

On the other hand, we can determine the most likely meaning of "Fix mechanic car," since a mechanic can fix something while a car must be fixed.

When experience can be brought to bear on an interpretation, sentences that are otherwise functionally ambiguous can be understood. Compare the following sentences:

John saw a meteor speeding through the sky.
John saw a mountain speeding through the sky.

These sentences have similar surface structures but different base structures. Most readers initially interpret the meteor to be speeding through the sky in the first sentence and John to be speeding through the sky (in a plane) in the second sentence. This interpretation is based on limited alternatives—me-

* Adapted from *An Introduction to Psychology*, by P. H. Lindsay & D. A. Norman. Copyright © 1972 by Academic Press, Inc. This and all other adaptations are used by permission.

teors always speed through the sky, John may speed through the sky, and mountains never speed through the sky.

Grammar is a remarkable tool for regularizing the process of communicating messages. Although people depart from grammatical rules in writing and speaking, they are still understood. By processing all contextual and experiential information, even messages that depart drastically from grammatical rules are almost always unravelled.

THE PSYCHOLOGICAL REALITY OF TRANSFORMATIONS

Transformational grammar relates the base structure of a sentence to its surface structure by a set of rules or operations. The more operations required to relate a sentence to its underlying meaning, the more complex the perceptual processing of the sentence becomes.

Growling lions raising flowers. The phrases "growling lions" and "raising flowers" seem to have the same surface structure. However, "growling lions" means "lions growl," while "raising flowers" means "they raise flowers." The second phrase has an extra *NP* that, though it is only implied, must be recognized by the reader or listener. Consider the tree structures shown in Figure 2–3.

Growling lions

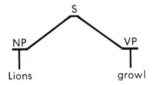

Raising flowers

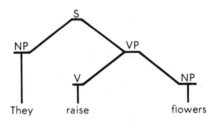

Figure 2-3. "Growling lions raising flowers."

The added noun phrase makes "raising flowers" more complex and therefore more difficult to understand than "growling lions" even though both have the same surface structure (Rohrman, 1968).

An early experiment.   Miller (1962) and his associates were among the first to study the relationship of transformations to the complexity of perceptual processing of sentences. In a typical experiment, the subject was given two columns of sentences. The sentences in the second column were transformed counterparts of those in the first column. For example, a sentence in the first column might have been the simple, affirmative, active, declarative sentence "Bozo liked the big bone." Its passive, "The big bone was liked by Bozo," would be presented somewhere in the second column. Other sentences represented negative and passive-negative transformations. The subject was told to find sentences related in certain ways to those in the first column—for example, given an affirmative sentence, he was told to find its negative counterpart. (Henceforth, such instructions will be represented as affirmative → negative; passive → active; passive → negative-passive; and so on.)

Some of the tasks were assumed to require only one operation— passive → negative-passive required applying only the negative transformation to the already passive sentence in the first column to find the correct sentence in the second column. Other tasks were assumed to require two transformations—negative → passive would require changing the negative sentence to an affirmative one and then applying the passive transformation to the active sentence. The number of grammatical operations was hypothesized to determine perceptual complexity, so the process of matching sentences requiring two transformational operations was predicted to take longer than the process of matching sentences requiring only one operation; indeed, these predictions were supported. The tasks involving searches for sentences corresponding to the single grammatical operations in active ↔ passive, passive ↔ passive-negative, and negative ↔ passive-negative each took about the same time. The search involving the assumed double operations for recognizing negative ↔ passive or active ↔ negative-passive sentences took about twice as long.

Other experiments relating assumed transformational operations to perceived complexity yielded similar results; this seems to support the psychological reality of transformations.

The case for semantics.   Recent evidence suggests that Miller's experimental results were ambiguous. Perceived complexity appears to be related to variables other than the number of operations; length and meaning co-vary with the number of grammatical operations, so perhaps these factors rather than the number of operations were responsible for Miller's results. For example, sentences assumed to require more operations (b) tend to be longer and have more complex meanings than those assumed to have fewer operations (a).

(a) Bill jumps.   (a) Mary is here.
(b) Does Bill jump?   (b) Isn't Mary here?

Accordingly, in either example, (a) may seem easier to recall or recognize because it is shorter rather than because fewer operations are involved.

Now examine another example, to extend the argument. The first sentence (a) below is shorter and grammatically simpler than the second sentence (b).

(a) John was hurt.
(b) John was hurt by someone.

Miller would have predicted that, because fewer operations are involved, (a) would be easier to understand than (b). In fact, evidence indicates the opposite—that (b) is easier to understand than (a)—and contradicts Miller's hypothesis. The relative ease of understanding (b) seems to be related to its being more meaningful, conveying a more precise meaning, and being psychologically less complex than (a) rather than to its relatively greater grammatical complexity and length. (These examples have been summarized from Fodor & Garrett, 1966, and Bever, 1970.)

Semantic strategies. No single factor or strategy explains how the meaning of a sentence is unravelled. Instead, evidence suggests that several strategies might be used, two of which will be illustrated from Bever's (1970) studies with children. A typical procedure in such a study is to present a sentence like one of those that follow to a child and ask him to act it out with toy objects.

(a) The mother pats the dog.
(b) The dog pats the mother.

Older children (3 to 5 years old) made more errors on the more improbable situation (b) than on the probable situation (a). Very young children (2 years old) are less affected by the differences in meaning since they base their interpretations on less experience than older children do. As a result, they do not know that people pat dogs but dogs do not pat people. After age 3, children begin to use a strategy for interpreting sentences that depends on identifying the more probable (sensible) semantic meanings.

When the meaning is not clear, a sentence might be interpreted by finding the agent, the action, and the object. This helps identify clauses, and even very young children are able to use this strategy, especially with active sentences. The same is true for the following sentences:

(a) It's the dog that chases the cat.
(b) It's the cat that the dog chases.

Four- and 5-year-olds perform (a) more accurately than (b), probably because the actor is first in (a) and last in (b). Although it is easier for older children and adults to find the meaning of such simple sentences, they, too, use this strategy. For example, adults are presented with the following sentences:

(a) Speedily the man took the car back.
(b) The man speedily took back the car.

When they are asked to recall them, nearly 90 percent of all errors are changes from (b) to (a); only 10 percent of the errors are changes from (a) to (b). In (a), the sequence of agent-action-object is clear, but in (b), the sequence is interrupted, so the hearer tends to impose the clearer structure on what he hears. So strong is this tendency that typists make many errors with the kind of material in (b), readers have difficulty in recalling the difference between (a) and (b) when they get beyond the examples, and uncautious writers may become trapped in their own examples.

An answer to the question. What determines the perceptual complexity of sentences? The relationship between number of transformational operations and perceptual complexity of sentences is not convincing. Grammar may represent the component parts of an utterance or sentence, but sentences are not always grammatical yet are still understood by both listener/reader and speaker/writer in the same way. The interpreter of the language seems to depend on both the structure of the sentence and on semantically sensible interpretations to arrive at a sentence's intended meaning.

LANGUAGE PROCESSING AND THE LEARNER

Transformational grammar's implications have resulted in a major realignment of psychological theories. The evidence indicates that language structures can be represented by rules. A person learning his first language acquires these structural rules by exposure to a variety of instances over time. Generalizations in the form of principles, rules, or operations are abstracted from these instances. In turn, they influence many aspects of behavior but it is not clear in which situations their influence is greatest.

Studying, learning, reviewing, and recalling are not simple input-output activities any more than using language is. Learning is a constant process that follows systematic rules; it is not capricious or random as many believed in an earlier era of psychology when trial-and-error theories were popular. We are only now beginning to understand that learners form a learning strategy; they reconstruct material, transforming sentences while reading or listening; they identify structures, reorganizing materials to suit their purposes; they make images, linking the material to what they already know; or they elaborate the material beyond what is given in a sentence. There are probably many other processes still waiting to be discovered.

PART
TWO
LANGUAGE AND
COGNITIVE DEVELOPMENT

CHAPTER
THREE
COGNITIVE
DEVELOPMENT

Chapter Three will discuss the development and use of words in the control of thought, the emergence of cognitive structures, and the distinction between competence and performance.

LANGUAGE AS A SIGNAL SYSTEM

Pavlov (1927) distinguished between the first and second signal systems. He noted that man has physical structures and reflexes similar to those of other animals. For example, man reacts to intense light by pupillary constriction and to a sudden, loud sound by the startle reflex; when man is severely threatened, his heart rate, blood-sugar levels, perspiration, and breathing all increase as adaptive devices. Pavlov called these built-in mechanisms the *first signal system*.

The first signal system functions on a biological level, but language also functions as a signal system. It enables man to regulate his own behavior or someone else's behavior. Language, then, radically changes the behavior of a biological organism. In Pavlov's terms, it forms the *second signal system*. As Pavlov said, "The word created a second system of signals of reality which is peculiarly ours, being the signal of signals. On the one hand, numerous speech stimuli have removed us from reality. . . . On the other, it is precisely speech which has made us human" (1927, p. 357). Pavlov implied that language produces profound quantitative and qualitative changes in man's behavior (Slobin, 1966).

Physically, man is not well adapted to his environment (Bruner, 1964); any one of his senses and physical abilities is surpassed by at least one other member of the animal kingdom. Man's use of his intellectual prowess together with his second signal system has enabled him to amplify his motor abilities (tools and machines), his senses (microscopes, amplifiers, and "sensing" devises), and his intellectual abilities (planning, programming for computers, and problem-solving). Most important, man has learned to use his intellectual abilities to help him understand how to strengthen his intellectual abilities.

WORDS AND BEHAVIOR

Words are used in most forms of communication among humans—in speaking, writing, reading, and listening. They are important not only to communicate meaning but also to label meaningful aspects of the environment and to manipulate ideas. Words provide at least a crude index of one's knowledge. Accordingly, an important index of one's cognitive ability is the size of one's vocabulary.

VOCABULARY GROWTH

Children's vocabularies increase dramatically from one word at 1 year to more than 2000 words at 5½ years (Smith, 1926). By adolescence, the vocabulary contains tens of thousands of words. At adolescence, the difference between basic (specific words with different meanings) and derived (different ways of expressing the same word) vocabularies may vary by as many as tens of thousands of words. First, there is a great difference between the number of words one understands in listening or recognizes in reading and the number of words one uses in speaking. Second, one's vocabulary varies according to his experience, with the artist having a larger vocabulary for his art than a mechanic does but the mechanic having a larger vocabulary for mechanics than the artist does. Third, vocabulary is related to one's knowledge of the language. Vocabulary increases geometrically: the more words one knows and the more he knows about how to use the language, the more his vocabulary and knowledge of the language are likely to increase. Fourth, individual differences determine inventive and metaphorical use of words; we may be able to understand such phrases as "the cancerous growth of a business," "the well of sorrow," "the river of life," or "ideas that are oceans apart," but we may not be able to originate them. Fifth, there are sex-related differences in vocabulary size; by all measures, girls have larger vocabularies than boys except possibly in certain areas such as outdoor activities or technical subjects, although evidence is lacking. Interestingly, vocabulary growth continues into old age although most physiological abilities and functions decline.

WORDS AND THE CONTROL OF BEHAVIOR

The Russian psychologist Luria was influenced by Pavlov's views. Luria's experiments were intended to demonstrate that, with increasing language experience, the child comes to have increasing control of his own behavior—that words control behavior. In the initial stages of development, the child comprehends the meaning of words such as go and stop, but they have no effect on his behavior. When he is told to "go," which in Luria's (1961) experiment meant to press a bulb, the child does so. But when he is told to "stop" in Luria's experiment, he continues to press the bulb. The command "stop" does not control his motor behavior until he has further experience. With increasing development, the child eventually learns to stop, or to release the bulb, on command. This research implies that understanding the language is different from using language to control behavior.

Control by words.   As a result of Luria's experiments, one can see how the control of behavior by language emerges. First, an understanding of the word is acquired. Second, the word has a general energizing function that activates a given behavior but does not limit it. When the child is told to stop pressing the bulb, he continues to press. Third, words acquire inhibitory functions. When told to "stop," the child does stop. As simple as the experiment appears to be, it does demonstrate how activation and inhibition, induced by language, lead to differentiated, precise behaviors.

So far, language has been shown to control motor processes by signals from an external source such as a teacher, parent, or experimenter. However, further training is required if language is to acquire self-regulatory functions. To respond to the command "stop," the child is trained to take his hand from the bulb and put his hand on the table. Until he does this, the child cannot use commands to himself to control his behavior. Eventually he can say "go" at the signal of a light or sound, at which time he will press the bulb. Then, he can say "stop" and will let the bulb go. When this stage is reached, language has a self-regulatory function. Luria's studies demonstrate the progressive differentiation of the ways language regulates behavior: first, knowing the meaning of the word; second, activating but not limiting behavior; third, controlling (activating and inhibiting) behavior by communication from an external source; and, fourth, self-regulation through instructions to oneself.

THE GROWTH OF COGNITIVE STRUCTURES

While Luria emphasized the meaning of words, the Swiss psychologist Jean Piaget emphasized that knowledge emerges in the form of cognitive structures—that cognition precedes thought. Piaget's early training as a biologist led him to link the development of knowledge to the total development of the body and of the nervous system.

The infant starts life with spontaneous movements and reflexes on which new habits and cognitions are built. The infant learns about his environment by building on these new habits and cognitions, not simply by absorbing information or by taking mental photographs. At first, thought arises from motor actions that are later transformed into mental activities, as we shall see in the following discussion (based on Piaget 1964 and 1969).

ADAPTATION: ACCOMMODATION AND ASSIMILATION

Actions are adaptive. When a child meets a new experience, he adjusts to it. As an infant, he pulls, grasps, pushes, or hits. When shaking his crib, the infant may see that a toy hanging from it moves. Later, he may deliberately shake his crib to make the toy move. These activities are the bases for interpreting the world about him in a process called *assimilation*, which means that a new experience is interpreted on the basis of whatever knowledge or ability a person (infant, child, or adult) has available to him. Causal relationships are represented in corresponding motor activity since this is the only knowledge structure available to the infant.

Not all experiences can be assimilated into a given knowledge structure. If growth in mental functions is to occur, mental structures must change. As increasingly complex relationships demand attention, the person must change his way of organizing knowledge. At first, the child understands the seesaw by motor activity. He adjusts the different weights almost at random. However, his understanding does not lead to efficient thinking. Sometime in the course of development, the child recognizes that differences in weight or differences in distance from the fulcrum have to be considered. His point of view has changed from motor activity to a concrete operation. With further development, the cognitive structures are modified to the point that the seesaw principle can be translated into the lever principle. Now the child's thought processes have changed so he can use formal logic and can express relationships in symbolic form: adjustments of the seesaw are based on considering the proportions of weight and length from the fulcrum in the form of $W_1/W_2 = L_2/L_1$. Clearly, change more than assimilation is involved in this example. A radical change in the child's way of organizing experience and way of thinking has occurred. The process of changing one's knowledge structure to explain experience is called *accommodation*.

To summarize, Piaget suggests that knowledge is organized around perceptions of differences, similarities, and relationships between events. Furthermore, knowledge is integrated around a view of the world that is characteristic for a given level of development. The integration has a pattern. As new experiences are encountered, the person adapts to them. The experience is modified either to conform to the individual's existing knowledge structure (assimilation) or the knowledge structure must be changed to account for the experience in a different way (accommodation).

STAGES OF COGNITIVE DEVELOPMENT

Operations, internalized as structures, constitute Piaget's definition of intelligence. We can look at these structures a little more closely by briefly outlining the four main stages described by Piaget.

The sensorimotor stage.   The first phase of cognitive development is the *sensorimotor or pre-verbal stage* (lasting from birth to 18 to 24 months). The child's knowledge during this phase is limited to his external activity. Simple movements, grasping, kicking, pushing, or looking take much of his time. Soon he may be attracted by an object some distance away and may move toward it, but he can easily be distracted by another object encountered enroute. His attention span is short and the immediate is more important than a long-range goal. Once an object is out of sight, it is out of mind; perhaps it is accurate to say that the child thinks the object has disappeared. Once that happens, he goes on to something else. The object has no permanence or stability for him.

With increasing experience, the beginnings of abstraction appear. Grasping, moving of arms, and looking become coordinated into hand-eye movements. The child has learned the beginnings of cause-and-effect relationships. He learns about the relationships of objects in space; they can be moved from one place to another, and he can control these movements. He has now learned that objects have permanence, and he has learned some elementary, practical cause-and-effect consequences of his activities. Such knowledge becomes the basis for later cognitive development.

The pre-operational stage.   The second phase of cognitive development is the *pre-operational stage* (lasting from 18 to 24 months to about 5 to 6 years). Language now begins to influence thought, and discoveries from the sensorimotor stage are represented in symbolic form. The child can now pretend he is asleep—a play activity that symbolizes sleep—whereas in the sensorimotor stage, *sleep* meant only the activity itself. He can pretend he is Daddy, also a symbolic activity—whereas in the sensorimotor stage, the word *Daddy* referred only to a specific person. He can also begin to express some simple relations, such as "to be big is to be tall." While clearly symbolic, this is an intuitive form of knowing since it does not fit all situations—for example, adults who are bigger are not necessarily taller.

The child in the pre-operational period is *egocentric*—that is, he cannot dissociate himself from external events. Egocentricity can be observed in the child's conversational activity, which is characterized by *echolalia*, or repeating his own phrases or sentences, and *monologue*, talking aloud to himself for his own benefit. When two or more children are playing with each other at the same task, each child may speak in turn. Although this has the appearance of a conversation since it is directed around the same activity, each child is carrying on his own monologue and does not respond to the other child's comments. This kind of interaction is called *collective monologue.*

Since the pre-operational child is egocentric, he may be unable to learn much by instruction. Communication through instruction requires receptivity and orientation to another's point of view, and these are obviously not the egocentric child's strong points.

Figurative and operational knowledge.   Between the discussions of the pre-operational and concrete-operations stages, two terms should be defined. *Operational knowledge* is the mental representation of manipulations that can be performed when the person is classifying events—that is, putting them into serial order or seeing relationships among them. To accomplish these operations he must rearrange objects, count, measure, and experiment. He may learn something about the physical characteristics of specific materials such as marbles or buckets of sand or, at a higher mental level, specific numbers, words, or pictures. This is *figurative knowledge*, but it is less important in Piaget's schema than that the actions on such items lead to a fundamental property of all cognitive functioning: structure, or organization. A number, for example, is not learned for its own sake (figurative knowledge) but in relation to other numbers that can be ordered in serial fashion—an operation. Later, numbers can be ordered more elegantly—in the context of algebra or calculus—using formal operations. Eventually, any area of knowledge gets intricately related with other areas, as mathematics does to physics, biology, chemistry, or even to the arts and the social sciences. Thus, any knowledge develops formal relationships to other knowledge.

The concrete-operations stage.   Piaget has performed many ingeniously contrived experiments to show how operations become internalized. One of these is called the conservation experiment. A typical task uses two containers such as glass tumblers that are filled to equal levels with water and sealed so they can't be spilled when tipped. The child is asked whether the tumblers contain the same amount of water. After careful inspection, he is typically satisfied that they do. Then one glass is laid on its side. The child is now asked whether one tumbler contains more, the same amount, or less water than the other tumbler. Inevitably, the child in the pre-operational stage will say the tumbler on its side contains less water than the upright tumbler. He will not conclude that both contain the same amount of water even if coaxed to do so. However, when both tumblers are brought again into upright position, he will agree that they contain the same amount of water. The same phenomenon can be demonstrated with two rectangular blocks of wood used in the same way as the tumblers; with two round balls of clay, one of which is rolled into a sausage; or with two rows of equal numbers of marbles, one row of which is elongated by adding more space between them. The result is always the same. If the child looks at length, he says, "more"; if he looks at thinness, lack of height, or density he says, "less"; but he never says "they are the same" unless they are brought back into the original positions or shapes. Thus, the child in the pre-operational stage cannot perform the operation of *reversibility* in order to conserve quantity. He lacks this ability because he focuses on only one dimension. This process is called *centration*. Conservation requires observing the change in relationships between two dimensions—that is, seeing that the change in height of water in the glass is compensated for by the change in its width. Using this process, called *decentration*, the child can consider both dimensions simultaneously.

The basic elements of mental operations appear in the third phase of cognitive development, the *concrete-operations stage* (lasting from 5 to 6 years to 11 to 12 years or older). When given the conservation tasks, the child at this stage of development responds correctly regardless of the position of the tumblers, the shape into which the ball is rolled, or the spacing of the marbles. Unlike the deliberative response of the pre-operational child, the child in the concrete-operations stage reflects certainty and boredom with the task. You can't shake him out of his decision that the two are the same. When presented with several tasks, his response suggests you are asking him to describe the obvious.

Other ingenious experiments have been performed to demonstrate the child's competence in using conceptual schemes. *Classification* structures are evaluated by using objects that vary on different dimensions such as shape, color, or size. Those with one characteristic (yellow color) are placed in one of two rings, and those with another characteristic (triangular shape) are placed in the other ring. All others are placed outside the two rings. The observer then asks the child where he would put a yellow triangle. By observing where it is placed, the observer can determine whether the child can make the classification and, if he can, on what basis (color or form) he makes the classification.

Probability structures are evaluated by similar tasks. The examiner might put 10 green gumdrops and one yellow gumdrop into a bag. Then the child is told that he can keep each gumdrop whose color he guesses correctly before drawing it from the bag without looking. Obviously, the best guess would be "green," but children typically make random guesses or, even if they make correct runs, will suddenly switch to the other color. This is a difficult task for children until late in the concrete-operations period.

During the concrete-operations period, children learn about abstractions as general ways of knowing—presumably, before they have mastered the meaningful use of language. At this stage, the fundamental operations of elementary science and mathematics are being formed. The child cannot perform these operations entirely through verbal means but must have concrete objects before him. Nevertheless, the child can use real operations— that is, he discovers structures that are distinct from the figurative properties of clay, water, or marbles. Thus, the operations become internalized in thought as structures. These operations become permanently learned and will not be forgotten.

The formal-operations stage. In the fourth phase of cognitive development, the *formal-operations stage* (lasting from 12 years through adulthood), the child can use reasoning based on logic, hypotheses, and deduction. He can represent knowledge in its most general form by language and other symbolic systems such as mathematics. Ideas can be related, differentiated, or combined mentally and logically through symbol systems. Maximum ability in formal operations (symbolic thinking) is probably achieved in early adulthood. However, since this is a period of mature thought, one may reasonably expect experiences throughout the life span to contribute to the growth of formal operations.

We can illustrate formal-operations intelligence by describing other Piagetian tasks. In one, the child may be given a balance scale on which he is to place weights in order to bring the two arms of the scale into equilibrium. In the early years, he knows that a weight has to be used, but he is not certain just where it is to be placed. Later, in the concrete-operations period, he knows that a heavier weight has to be used on the side that is higher. He focuses on one dimension but does not take distance from the fulcrum into account. In the later part of the formal-operations period, his behavior suggests that he understands the idea of the proportion involved ($W_1/W_2 = L_2/L_1$). He can now deal with the problem symbolically as well as in a practical way.

Another of Piaget's tasks is the pendulum problem, in which the child is to determine the factor that makes the pendulum go faster. In the initial developmental stages, the child cannot tell whether it is weight or the length of the string that makes the difference. Later he recognizes that the pendulum's speed is determined by the length of the string; the shorter the string, the faster the pendulum goes.

With verbal problems, the concrete-operations child has difficulty with assumptions. If you were to begin a problem with the assumption, "Suppose the sun did not give light or heat," the child would say, "The sun does give light and heat, so you can't answer the problem." The child in the formal-operations period can deal with assumptions. He recognizes that the logic involved takes precedence over the validity of assumptions stated as assumptions.

In other verbal problems, the child might be given a statement of relations such as:

> John is taller than Bill. John is shorter than Harry. Who is the tallest?

This kind of problem requires two assumptions to be kept in mind and then related to each other in a third operation. In the concrete-operations period, the child can deal with only two ideas and cannot solve the problem. In the formal-operations period, he can deal successfully with all three ideas and can solve the problem.

Only about 50 percent of the population in the United States reaches the level of mature formal-operational thought (Kohlberg & Mayer, 1972).

LANGUAGE AND COGNITIVE DEVELOPMENT

Piaget's theory shows the transition from the infant's apparently random bodily movements to his complicated use of language in thought. The child is not simply a passive organism responding to any stimuli that occur. He is an active, adaptive organism behaving in a very complicated way. Other transitions from any of the stages to the next are just as remarkable. The changes in the way the child perceives, represents, and operates on the world appear to emerge in very regular and systematic ways analogous to the regularity of biological and language-structure development.

CONSERVERS AND NON-CONSERVERS

Some investigators (Bruner, Olver, & Greenfield, 1966) have argued that language can be used to facilitate changes from one stage to another. They say that language can help the child focus on structures (classifications based on object functions, such as furniture, toys, books, and so on) rather than their perceptual attributes (such as height or color). However, if the child has not attained a sufficient level of comprehension, special training is ineffective.

Differences in the child's ability to use language appear in the language of conservers and non-conservers. When asked to differentiate between two objects such as a matchbox and a piece of chalk, conservers tend to express *relations*, such as "one is larger than the other" or one is "more round than the other," more than do non-conservers. Conservers also tend to use more pairs of precise terms that express *differentiations*, such as *dark* and *light* and *long* and *short*, rather than unrelated terms, such as *fat* and *short*. Finally, conservers tend to use *coordinated* characteristics in parallel fashion, such as "The box is shorter but fatter; the chalk is longer but skinnier." When children are explicitly taught to use these terms, differentiation is learned first, then relations, and coordination last. But teaching these forms of language expression does not guarantee that children will be able to use them in other situations; children who had not yet reached the conservation stage were found to be unable to transfer their newly acquired knowledge to other tasks.

DIAGONAL AND NON-DIAGONAL CHILDREN

Another study shows the relationship between language and cognitive development. Olson (1970b) found that most 4- to 5-year-olds could look at a diagonal in one figure and select its counterpart from alternatives including a straight line across the top of a square and another down the side of the square. Of those who performed the task successfully, many were unable to reproduce the diagonal with checkers on a checkerboard from a corresponding display of checkers arranged into a diagonal on a checkerboard. Thus, the ability to recognize the diagonal and the ability to reproduce it are not identical skills at the pre-school level. This difference in abilities emphasizes the developmental lag between perceiving and performing.

What does the child who can reproduce diagonals know that the child who cannot does not know? Olson inferred that the diagonal child knew a conceptual system something like, "A diagonal is a crisscross. It starts at a corner. It goes straight across the middle of the board. It ends at the other corner." In effect, this is a set of rules for combining critical alternatives that produce only the diagonal.

Verbal instruction about the structure does help the non-diagonal child. For variety, different statements of the rules were used such as, "Pretend the checkers are stepping stones, how would you get from here to here?" To compare the effectiveness of this approach, other children were taught by reinforcement (trial-and-error) techniques. These children took twice as long to learn the task, ten times as many trials during learning, and twice as many trials on a transfer task (starting at the other corner) than did the children who were instructed about the structure. The trial-and-error procedure depended on reinforcement of specific responses, and even when the children learned to make the diagonal in this way they learned specific, independent responses; they did not seem to know how to put the checkers down in sequence according to the system of rules.

Even when verbally instructed about the structure, some children who could recite the verbal concept, define the diagonal, and draw it still could not reproduce it on the checkerboard. Thus, language was not a sufficient means of instruction. An important prerequisite is the ability of the child to perceive the essential features that comprise the system rather than to perceive only the end-product. Once the child has learned to identify the critical features, language codes can be associated with them. When this occurs, verbal instruction is efficient.

Cognitive development proceeds as an elaboration of the child's perceptual knowledge (of features he must recognize) in the course of performing his activities. As his perceptual world becomes increasingly differentiated, the child learns which attributes are important—that is, he learns which alternatives are available and, of these, which ones are correct.

To some extent, the culture provides perceptual experience that makes some tasks easier than others. In extensions of his studies, Olson found that many children in Kenyan tribes in East Africa were unable to reproduce the diagonal even when they were 9 years old. An examination of the tribal culture shows why. In that part of Africa there is little opportunity for experience with the spatial and geometric discriminations required for such activities as measuring, building, and engineering. They simply are not needed there. Furthermore, there is an absence of rectangularity in that culture in contrast to our fenced-off fields, our rectangular city blocks, or our carpentered and engineered architecture. Since spatial discriminations are relatively unnecessary, they are not coded in the language and, of course, are not articulated by the adults. In fact, the only word that is related to the diagonal system is *kona*, meaning *corner*, and that word was borrowed from the English.

The Kenyan child's ability to reproduce the diagonal was correlated with number of years of schooling. In the United States it was not. By the time the child enters school in the United States, he has learned whatever perceptual alternatives are essential to learning the diagonal. He knows that *corner* is different from the perceptual alternatives of *middle* or *edge*. He knows that crisscross means corner-to-corner across the middle, and that this is perceptually different from the alternatives *edge to edge, across the top*, or *top to bottom*. Schooling contributes little more to these distinctions. On the other hand, the Kenyan child acquires this information gradually from the formal curriculum as he proceeds through the grades. Thus, the demands of the culture (in terms of its differentiations and organization of features) determine how the child's perceptual world will be elaborated.

LANGUAGE AND INSTRUCTION

Olson's studies have several implications for instruction:

1. The child's performance in selecting perceptual alternatives is a critical feature on which the teacher should focus as the child learns.

2. At critical choice points, where conflict is encountered, the learner can be led to seek further information. Verbal instruction might be used to replace activity if language has become functional to the child.

3. Reinforcement in the strict sense of operant conditioning (trial and error) will be ineffective unless the child views the experience as an instance of the correct alternative—that is, if the child focuses on the right feature. Non-reinforcement of incorrect alternatives and choices can help the child make contrasts with the correct, or reinforced, feature; however, the very young child does not ordinarily take advantage of this opportunity.

4. Language can be an important medium of instruction, but its use with children is limited to the aspects of language the child can understand.

5. Even more important, the teacher must know whether the child defines ideas he understands in the same way adults define them. Olson illustrates this difference by a description attributed to Piaget:

Teacher: Why does a boat float?
Pupil: Because if it sank all the people would drown.

Thus, the child's comprehension of language can differ in both the meaning and use of words from adult comprehension.

6. Finally, while language is flexible, in many situations language is unsuitable and other media—perhaps a visual aid or an activity—are necessary. Verbal description may help in performing a skill and for selecting some of the alternatives but it is never the same as doing the activity.

Olson's work implies that activity is essential in the early years of schooling, as does Piaget's work. The Montessori method seems to fulfill the requirements of Piaget's and Olson's ideas equally well, as would any teaching method that requires activity; instruction in the elementary school cannot be exclusively verbal.

The end of the formal-operations stage marks the point of mature cognitive development. Other features of development—including general maturation, social development, learning, and equilibration—have contributed to this attainment. At the time the child reaches the formal-operations stage, he can profit from the most efficient form of instruction—verbal instruction.

At each level of development, language is used for instruction although it is not equally efficient nor used in the same way by teacher and pupil at each level. At first, language may be used for descriptive purposes such as naming or pointing. Only later does it become effective for thinking and reasoning, which can be predicted by the learner's level of cognitive development rather than his chronological age.

COMPETENCE AND PERFORMANCE

Piaget distinguished between competence and performance in the tasks he devised for measuring the child's cognitive capacities. This distinction has been revived in current approaches to psycholinguistics.

The child develops a set of language rules that enable him to speak, understand, and otherwise communicate. By the time he enters school, he has had literally thousands of experiences in this process. He hears others and he is heard. He names objects and objects are named for him. He is requested to perform tasks and he requests others to perform tasks. He receives commands and he gives them. He is asked questions and he asks questions. For some of these utterances, he is reinforced mostly by obtaining uniform and predictable responses such as answers to his questions or receiving the objects he requested. He may not be reinforced for other utterances—that is, he is likely to be corrected either verbally or by not getting the response he wanted. The child constructs his grammar by abstracting common rules (structures) out of these varied experiences. Discrepancies will be modified with continuing experience until they disappear so that language usage conforms to that of the language community.

COMPETENCE VERSUS PERFORMANCE

At any stage of development, then, a person: has a vocabulary; uses different rules for forming declarative or interrogative, active or passive, and affirmative or negative sentences; knows something about what different stresses, intonations, and expressions mean; can understand much more than he can use or produce. This is his *competence.* It reflects his ability, which is acquired from experience and is tempered somewhat by innate ability and the characteristics of his nervous system. As far as we know, all children proceed through similar stages in linguistic development—that is, the order in which certain constructions and speech forms occur is uniform for all children. The age at which a given stage of linguistic competence is reached varies from child to child, depending on such variables as native endowment and experience.

Competence can be measured only through *performance,* or the productions of the speaker. This is true even for intuitive conclusions about grammar. Researchers are seeking other measures that reflect competence but such measures are difficult to develop for young children, whose language development is undergoing rapid, important changes.

MEASURING PERFORMANCE AND INFERRING COMPETENCE

The corpus. Grammatical competence has been studied by collecting a *corpus* (a very complete sample) of all words or sentences produced by a child, usually during the first years of life. Such longitudinal samples are useful since they can reflect growth changes; the disadvantage of this approach is that the occasion for using some rules may never arise in natural discourse or may occur so infrequently that they are missed by the observer. Collections of spontaneous speech, therefore, are somewhat unreliable. Other measures, such as length of sentences, are also inadequate because they may be too superficial and therefore misleading; for example, long sentences can be constructed by using conjunctions to string ideas out, one after another. Such sentences can be shortened by deleting some of the conjunctions or using commas and deletion rules. The shorter sentence in this instance indicates greater competence because it reflects the use of additional operations.

Donald and Bozo. C. Chomsky (1969) has developed the most effective procedures for distinguishing between competence and performance. She interviewed children by asking relatively complex questions (for children 5 to 10 years old) that required the application of a transformational rule to make a correct interpretation. The children were shown two toy figures, Donald and Bozo, and were instructed as follows:

1. Donald *tells* Bozo to lie down. Make him do it.
2. Donald *promises* Bozo to lie down. Have him do it.

In (1), the minimal distance principle (MDP) (Rosenbaum, 1967; C. Chomsky, 1969) applies. The implicit subject of the complement verb *to lie* is the noun phrase *Bozo* immediately preceding it. This rule applies to most sentences in which the main verb commands or requests. *To lie* is the complement of both main verbs *tells* and *promises*. However, when the main verb is *promises*, the rule must be changed to: violate the MDP and assign the first noun phrase *Donald* as subject to the complement verb *to lie* (see C. Chomsky, 1969, pp. 9–12). Because of this required change in the rule, (2) represents a more complex syntactical structure than (1). Accordingly, C. Chomsky hypothesized that younger children would respond correctly to (1) and incorrectly to (2), while older children would respond correctly to both sentences; that is, in (1), the child would make Bozo lie down while in (2), the child would make Donald lie down. Her findings supported her hypothesis.

Is the doll hard/easy to see?   C. Chomsky also used other tasks to determine the child's understanding of the base structure of sentences that have identical surface structures, such as:

> John is eager to please.
> John is easy to please.

Both the surface structure and the base structures are the same in the first sentence; the first noun, following standard grammar, takes precedence as the subject. *Eager* is predicated of John. It is John who is eager; he is the performer. In the second sentence, the function of the first noun is changed. A grammatical operation is needed. *John* is the object of *easy to please*; he is being acted upon.

Because of the differences between surface and base structures in such sentences, C. Chomsky hypothesized that a greater knowledge of syntax would be required to understand the meaning of the second sentence than the first sentence. She reasoned that very young children, because of their immature language development, would have more difficulty following directions based on the second construction than on the first.

In order to test this hypothesis she placed a blindfolded doll before the child who served as a subject and asked the child:

> Is the doll easy to see?
> Is the doll hard to see?

All of the 5-year-old children said the doll was "hard to see," and all of the 9-year-old children said it "was easy to see." The 6-, 7-, and 8-year-old children gave mixed responses. Furthermore, all of the children who had said that the doll was "hard to see," when asked to make the doll "easy to see," removed the blindfold from the doll.

Similar misunderstandings occur in the use of relational phrases based on *before* and *after* (Clark & Clark, 1968). *Before* is more easily understood than *after* by 3-year-old children in a sentence such as

> Move the red plane before/after you move the green plane.

Other investigators (Donaldson & Balfour, 1968; Palermo, 1973) have found that even up to age 7, some children used the two relational terms *more* and *less* synonymously in tasks such as adding water to jars or taking water from jars. For these children, *more* is *less*.

Can a child comprehend? These results indicate that the child's interpretation of meaning does not correspond directly to his ability to use words, and the elementary school child's comprehension is limited by his cognitive capacity. The shift in ability to use words for expressing relations in the production and comprehension of sentences seems to occur in the transition from the pre-operational stage to the concrete-operations stage, which again indicates that verbal instruction may not be very effective in elementary school. During this period, the child is learning how to use the language, but this is not to say that he can use the language effectively. The meanings of given words in their concrete or abstract (even metaphorical) use, the semantic relations among words, the syntactic features (markers) for given words, and the syntax of sentences all contribute to comprehension and are yet to be learned.

Nevertheless, children do try to interpret sentences. By selecting constructions of increasing difficulty, the investigator can measure the extent of the child's comprehension. By identifying where in the hierarchy of syntactical structures the child's understanding falters (that is, by evaluating the child's performance) the investigator can infer the level of the child's competence. Comparative studies of children in different age groups will eventually lead to a clearer understanding of the linguistic competencies associated with a given age and of the order in which syntactical structures emerge. On this basis alone, the distinction between competence and performance seems justified.

CHAPTER
FOUR
LANGUAGE
ACQUISITION

It is difficult to determine precisely when the child knows most of the fundamental rules of the language system. The decision depends on the criteria used. If the criterion is the child's first use of functionally complete (but not necessarily grammatically correct) sentences, then he knows the rules when he is about 3 years old. On the other hand, if the criterion is the child's use of more sentences that are grammatically correct than incorrect, then he knows the rules when he is about 5 years old. At 5 years, the child has also acquired the basic lexicon; language development, as opposed to acquisition, proceeds as the lexicon is enlarged and sentence structure is elaborated.

McNeill, for example, says, "Grammatical speech does not begin before 1½ years of age; yet as far as we can tell, the basic process is complete by 3½ years. Thus, a basis for the rich and intricate competence of adult grammar must emerge in the short span of 24 months. . . . Add to rapid acquisition the further fact that what is acquired is knowledge of abstract linguistic structure . . . [and we see how amazing it is that children learn to speak in such a short time]" (McNeill, 1966, p. 15). The rapidity of language acquisition and development is explained by three factors. First, the pre-school child has had no previous language experience to interfere with his learning, as, for example, does the child learning a second language; second, the verbalizations of others around him probably comprise a major source of environmental stimulation, although the child still experiences only a fragment of all possible sentences that he will eventually be capable of understanding and generating in the future. Third, language continues to develop for another 10 or 15 years after the beginning of elementary school.

THE PROGRESSION OF
LANGUAGE DEVELOPMENT

What is the child doing when he learns the language? He is of course learning to make appropriate sounds. Basic sounds are formed into combinations roughly equivalent to words. Initially, a single word can indicate a number of base structures, and later two or three words are combined in ways that reflect crude grammatical classes and the beginnings of sentences. Finally, the sentences become more complex.

Table 4–1 is a general description of the stages of language development. It is based on Menyuk's (1971) summary of experimenters' observations. (Note that the times indicated are approximate. They should not be construed as normative periods.)

Table 4–1. The sequence of emerging language behaviors.

Birth to 6 months	*The infant period.* The child produces such sounds as grunts, cries, gasps, shrieks, chuckling, and cooing (at 4 months).
6 months to 9 months	*The babbling period.* The child produces units of utterances called babbling that differ from one situation to another. These units begin to be acoustically similar to adult utterances because the child sloughs off the irrelevant phonemes rather than acquiring new phonemes.
9 months	*The jargon period.* Stresses and intonation patterns in strings of utterance units clearly correspond to those of the adult. Some imitation of general language-like patterns can be identified. Specific morphemes cannot be distinguished easily by the listener.
9 months to 1 year	*The quiet period.* The decrease in vocalization during this period of development is interesting. Language habits continue to develop but changes are not immediately apparent to the observer. One reason for this period of relative quiet may be the discontinuity in language development between the previous stage and next stages; a transition occurs from the use of jargon to the use of words as the adult knows them.
1 year to 2 years	*The holophrastic stage.* The child uses single words to indicate whole phrases. He can use base structure, but transformational rules to produce the surface structure have not been acquired. The single word is the start of the child's vocabulary. Pre-conventional "words" are considered words by the parent because a given sound pattern is used consistently in similar situations (for example, using "muk" for milk). These vocalizations sound like words and may be considered words by the prideful parents.

The child understands much of what he is told. He demonstrates his comprehension by responding in a way that is meaningful to the adult—he may obey a command or point to an object.

At the end of this period, the child produces from 20 words (at about 18 months) to 200 words (at about 21 months). |
| 2 years | *The spurt in word development.* Many conventional words appear in the child's vocabulary, which increases from 300 to 400 words at 24 to 27 months to 1000 words at 36 months. He |

produces two- and three-word utterances, phrases, and sentences in which the pivot-open structure is well established.

A given word can be used with a number of intonations: specifically, declarative ("doll."); emphatic ("doll!"); and interrogative ("doll?").

3 years

The sentence period. At 36 to 39 months, the child can use 1000 words; he uses sentences containing grammatical features that anticipate the adult's use of language rules. He uses functionally complete sentences—that is, sentences that clearly designate an idea as in the sentence, "This one riding horse." —that are grammatically incomplete.

3 to 5 years

The child uses sentences of all types: non-understandable sentences, functionally complete but grammatically incomplete sentences, simple sentences, simple sentences with phrases, compound sentences, complex sentences, and compound-complex sentences.

5 years to maturity

The individual's language system shows more frequent use of sentences with complex structure, increases in the variety of types of sentences, and increases in the length of sentences.

Language rules are learned in relatively distinct stages following a clearly defined sequence. While one stage regularly precedes another for all children, not all children reach each stage at the same age.

BABBLING

During the babbling period, sounds characteristic of the language are acquired. Although the infant can produce all the sounds of any language during his first few months of life, by the age of 6 or 7 months, he has *sloughed off* any sounds that are irrelevant or unnecessary in his language. At this age, a skilled observer who listens to the babbling of babies from different language communities can identify the different sounds (somewhat akin to phonemes) they produce.

With this accomplishment behind him, the quiet period begins at around 9 months. This is a transition period during which the fundamentals of language structure are being acquired. The child is learning that words mean something and can change others' behavior. At the end of the quiet period, at about 1 year, a new word or two appears in the child's speech; it may be a standard word or it may only approximate a standard word. Nevertheless, it is used in certain predictable kinds of situations and no others.

THE HOLOPHRASTIC PERIOD

The first words used by the child are holophrases—single words with many meanings that are used to meet different demands. The child may say "truck," meaning that a truck just drove into his driveway, that he wants his toy truck, or that a truck is passing the car in which he is riding: he is using a word to express a meaning. The holophrase anticipates the development of the surface structures of language. At this very early age, the child has learned a rule of the language.

TELEGRAPHIC SPEECH AND PIVOT-OPEN STRUCTURES

At about 20 months, two-word utterances resembling telegraphic speech make their appearance. (Telegraphic speech is analogous to writing a telegram in which many words are omitted, leaving only the key words.) By counting the different words used in the first and second place of a two-word utterance, early investigators inferred some rules that might characterize the child's language at this stage (Braine, 1963; Brown & Fraser, 1964; Miller & Ervin, 1964). Their theory, known as *pivot-open grammar*, was based on sets of words that were used with different degrees of frequency. Pivot-class (*P*) words consisted of a small class of frequently used words, such as *allgone, bye-bye,* and *more.* Open-class (*O*) words consisted of a larger set of infrequently used words, such as *boy, shoe, Mommy, milk,* and *truck.* The phrases (*S*) constructed by the child during the two-word utterance stage were supposedly characterized by the rule:

$S \rightarrow (P) + O.$
$P \rightarrow$ allgone, bye-bye, more . . .
$O \rightarrow$ boy, shoe, milk, Mommy, book, truck . . .

Any of the pivot words are combined with open words, but they are rarely used alone or in combinations with other pivot words. The open words are used alone or combined with a pivot word or another open word. Thus, such combinations as "allgone truck" ($S \rightarrow P + O$), "Mommy book" ($S \rightarrow O + O$), or "milk" ($S \rightarrow O$) are more likely than "allgone" ($S \rightarrow P$) by itself or "allgone more" ($S \rightarrow P + P$).

The pivot-open grammar points to regularities in the child's speech. However, its emphasis on form, frequency, and arrangement of words ignores syntactic and semantic rules that the child might be using. While it may describe the child's first use of two-word utterances, it does not adequately consider the child's comprehension. In fact, later analyses indicate that this theory's restrictions are violated by most children in the two-word stage.

As a result of such criticisms, some investigators have called the pivot-open grammar a false lead (Brown, 1973a). Others have shown that even the earliest two-word utterances contain grammatical relations, one word referring to the topic and the other modifying it (McNeill, 1970). Small words—such as auxiliary verbs, prepositions, and conjunctives, sometimes called *functors*—are omitted, perhaps because of their slight phonetic substance, minimal stress, complexity, or slight semantic modulations (such as number, time, and exactness) (Brown & Bellugi, 1964; Brown, 1973a). Thus, these first strings of words do follow the general form of the sentence and the words are ordered appropriately according to the adult's use of the language.

LEARNING TO COMMUNICATE MEANING

Understanding language means understanding the semantic relationships expressed by language (see Fillmore, 1968). Some of these relationships will be discussed next.

Verbs indicate action:

John *hit* Bill.

The noun *John* indicates who is performing the action—*John* is the agent. The other noun, *Bill*, indicates the recipient of the action.

How the action was performed is an instrumental relation:

John hit Bill *with* a ball.

A conditional relation indicates the condition under which the action occurs:

John hit Bill *because* he was angry.

Locative relations indicate where the action took place:

John hit Bill *on* the playground.

Possessive relations indicate who owns a characteristic:

John's anger is upsetting.

Reference relations name an event:

That is John.
That is a circus.

These relationships are largely expressed by functors—small words such as *in, up, as, the,* and *by.* Without these words, the semantic structure can be communicated only if the order of the words or the context in which the communication occurs are reliable.

CONTEXT AND LANGUAGE STRUCTURES

Since many early investigators were interested only in linguistic analyses, they had limited, inadequate interpretations of children's speech. Within their framework, the absence of functors required description of some assumed grammar, such as the pivot-open grammar, to the neglect of semantics. Bloom (1970) was among the first investigators of language development to consider semantics. She transcribed the child's utterances together with their contexts. Rather than chronological age, she used the *mean length of utterance* (MLU, based on the number of words spoken) developed by Brown and Fraser (1963) as an index of language development. Bloom's observations were based on children whose MLU was between 1.0 and 2.0 words (their chronological ages ranged from 19 to 23 months). She found that identical utterances could be interpreted differently by considering their contexts. Thus the phrase "Mommy sock" might suggest a possessor-possessed relationship (the child picks up the mother's sock) or an agent-object relationship (the mother puts a sock on the child). Clearly, the child is doing more than naming successive events; he is expressing some relationship.

More recently, Brown (1973a, 1973b) emphasized the complexity of both syntax and semantics in language acquisition. His theoretical framework presents five stages, the first when the MLU is between 1.0 and 2.0 and succeeding stages represented by increments of 0.5 MLUs.

SEMANTIC RELATIONSHIPS

In the first of Brown's stages of language development, utterances appear to be related to sensorimotor activities. Increases in MLU during this stage are due primarily to two-term utterances becoming three- and four-term utterances. Brown has hypothesized that these utterances express 18 relationships during Stage I, including some of the examples that follow:

Kind of relation	*Example*
reference (naming)	"that ball"

recurrence (requesting a reappearance)	"more ball"
possessive	"Daddy chair"
locative (location)	"book table"
experiencer-state	"I hear"
instrumental	"sweep broom"
agent-object	"Daddy ball"
agent-action	"Daddy hit"
action-object	"hit ball"

Longer sentences are based on the same structures. Three-term and four-term utterances, in effect, combine the relations expressed in the simpler two-term utterances. Thus the child may say "Adam hit ball," which can be represented as agent + action + object. It is constructed as if the child combined agent + action ("Adam hit") and action + object ("hit ball") into one sequence, but the action ("hit") is not repeated.

FUNCTIONAL RELATIONSHIPS

In the later stages of language development (beginning at the second stage), functional morphemes are incorporated into the child's language system. These include noun and verb inflections, prepositions, and articles, which generally must be used to produce a correct sentence. For example, for "Book," spoken in the context of pointing, an article is required; "Here two book" requires a plural inflection; and in "I running," an auxiliary, *am*, must be used. Note that it may not be essential to express all relations. Some may be optional in describing an event. Consider the following sentence:

John put the picture on the wall.

It represents an agent + object + location relation. The use of the word *put* requires that an indication of location must be used. However, other relations such as possessor (whose picture?), time (when was the picture put on the wall?), or instrument (how was the picture put on the wall?) are not necessary for this message. In another message, these relationships might be stated:

Today, John nailed Jill's picture of the windmill on the living-room wall.

However, the original sentence does not require them.

The acquisition of functors occurs gradually, increasing slowly throughout the five MLU stages. Use of functional morphemes is more highly correlated with MLU (the correlation is .92) than with age (the correlation is .68), which indicates that increases in the complexity of language usage are better predicted by developmental stages than by chronological age (Brown, 1973a).

TAG QUESTIONS

A third major stage in language acquisition reported by Brown (Brown, 1973b; Brown & Hanlon, 1970) is the beginning of use of tag questions. As they are used by adults, these questions are semantically simple but grammatically complex. As requests for confirmation, they are appended to declarative statements:

> John will be late, won't he?
> Mary can't drive, can she?

The initial semantics of the tag as simple requests for confirmation are acquired at the time the child uses two-word utterances. He may say, for example, "okay?" or "right?" but he does not use the well-formed, longer tags just cited. These more complex tags do not appear until several years later because their use seems to require understanding of a number of rules: (1) using the pronoun of the subject, (2) changing the verb to the opposite of that used in the declarative statement, (3) reversing the order of the verb and subject, and (4) making the tag a question (see Brown, 1973a, pp. 103–104). These observations suggest that language structures are acquired in the order of their grammatical complexity.

IS LANGUAGE LEARNED
BY IMITATION?

Clearly, language is not learned solely by imitation. The child forms rules to generate new sentences rather than only imitating the sentences used by others. At 18 months, a child cannot be enticed into repeating in full a sentence such as "The truck has gone." He may say "truck gone" or "allgone truck," but he is not likely to repeat the entire sentence. The child is using his own rules for constructing sentences and for interpreting them. Perhaps at this level of development he does not hear the other words in the sentence. Adults who pronounce *thing* as *ting* exhibit a similar phenomenon. When told, "It is pronounced *thing*, not *ting*," they hear it as, "It is pronounced *ting*, not *ting*,"; what they hear is congruent with their rule for language production.

No person, child or adult, repeats the same utterances in exactly the same form from one occasion to the next. Even when reading from a printed text, some interpretation or elaboration, consistent with one's experiential history, is likely to be made. Exact repetitions occur only in contrived laboratory experiments or other limited situations. More typically, language is used in a variety of ways to express one's ideas; paraphrase and other forms of interpretation are more often the rule than the exception. The ultimate forms such expressions take are derived from one's own frame of reference —that is, from the grammatical rules with which the speaker-listener is familiar.

LANGUAGE UNIVERSALS

So far, chapter Four has shown that the sequence of language development is regular enough to be described. This regularity suggests that humans may have innate structures for learning language—not a particular language, of course, but any language. Language acquisition is the product of these innate structures, maturation, and experience. More explicitly, language acquisition is the result of: (1) the functions or *characteristics of the nervous system* that permit the acquisition of grammatical rules; (2) the *content of the grammar* as represented in the specific language community where it is being acquired; (3) the *psychological processes* underlying the ability to use the system; and (4) the *stages* through which linguistic ability emerges in its progress to maturity.

The language of a given community is the result of these elements. The mature speaker in that community has a highly distinctive and complex set of linguistic rules at his command. These rules are not so abstract that they cannot be acquired by all members of the community. Obviously, with appropriate training, the language rules for one community can be acquired by members of any other language community. There are remarkable consistencies in the grammatical rules for the more than 2000 past and present languages. Chomsky and other linguists have inferred from these consistencies that there is a set of *language universals* that reflect innate structures.

SOME LANGUAGE UNIVERSALS

There are many regularities in language. (1) Every language has a phonological system. All language communities develop speech patterns that are basic sounds combined into morphemes. It is true that across different language communities the number of phonemes varies, as does the number of morphemes, but there is always a consistent set of phonological rules for expressing surface structures in speech, whether the community has developed in isolation or not. (2) Every community, too, has nouns and verbs. Some communities lack functors, such as some of the prepositions or auxiliaries, but the content parts of speech are always there. (3) In the construction of sentences, several combinations of subject-verb-object relationships are possible. Nevertheless, no more than three of the combinations have been found across all language communities. (4) Similarly, all languages use the basic syntactic categories of noun phrases and verb (predicate) phrases. (5) Finally, every language has describable rules for transforming the base structure from one surface structure into another.

DOES LANGUAGE DEVELOPMENT
HAVE A BIOLOGICAL BASE?

Other observations suggest the universal nature of language. First, its regular development can be identified by appropriate observational techniques. The orderly emergence of language is characteristic of all children in all language communities. Second, adults from a variety of backgrounds, whether native or foreign, who speak English are relatively consistent about their intuitions regarding the grammaticality of sentences.

These observations have led psycholinguists to suggest that language acquisition may proceed in a biologically determined way. The emergence of speech and language is correlated with physical development, even for retarded children (Lenneberg, 1969). Language development, though influenced by degree of exposure to the language, follows a describable course. As Lenneberg notes, it does not occur before or after a given period of development. It cannot be held back. Children from impoverished environments have been found to construct grammatically correct sentences to which they could never have been exposed.

Deaf children who are first taught language when they are in school come to the language late and have difficulty learning the syntax. They must learn it as a second language, which puts them at a disadvantage (Lenneberg, 1969). This suggests a possible critical period (a "best" time) for acquiring language.

THE LANGUAGE ACQUISITION
DEVICE

In order to consider the possible innate characteristics of language development, a Language Acquisition Device (LAD) has been proposed as a model of how language might be acquired (Chomsky, 1965; Katz, 1966; McNeill, 1966, 1971). Note that this model says the child behaves as if LAD existed; the model does not imply that LAD really exists—in fact, McNeill cautions that LAD is a fictitious aid for thinking about language. LAD consists of the assumed mechanisms, or innate schemata, that are built into the organism. It permits the detection of certain properties of the language over others and is analogous to a concept- or rule-formation mechanism. Thus, LAD consists of language universals—both identified and yet unidentified universals.

One way to view LAD is as a state of the organism that permits the learner to profit in certain ways from experience. Figure 4–1 shows the mediating function of LAD in relation to the environment and to language competence or performance. LAD enables the child to sift out the relevant features of experience and form relationships among these features—that is, it helps him to identify the rules comprising the language system. Continual recycling achieves closer approximations to the language community's accepted usage.

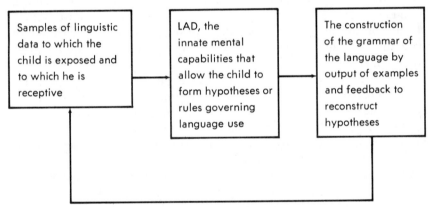

Figure 4-1. Language Acquisition Device (LAD).

Lenneberg and Piaget suggest that experiences are analyzed and resynthesized; consequently, the state of the organism is changed so that it becomes receptive to different experiences or aspects of experience.

The continuing spiral of experience and receptivity is called *epigenesis*. Referring to language, Lenneberg says, "The child [may] first react only to intonation patterns. With continued exposure to these patterns as they occur in a given language, mechanisms develop that allow him to process the patterns and in most instances to reproduce them. . . . This changes him so that he reaches a new state, a new potential for language development. Now he becomes aware of certain articulatory aspects, can process them and possibly reproduce them, and so on. A similar sequence of acceptance, synthesis, and state of new acceptance can be demonstrated on the level of semantics and syntax" (Lenneberg, 1969, p. 641). Thus, knowledge of the language comes from the "initially given structures of the mind" interacting with maturational processes and environmental experience.

LEARNING LANGUAGE RULES
COMPARED TO FORMAL INSTRUCTION

Language development is related to biological development. When it comes to learning the rules of language, the child is especially inventive and creative. He can and will make rules, a behavioral tendency of all human beings. In order to construct highly generalized rules the child is exposed to a variety of utterances—that is, a *corpus* of utterances—which, though numerous, are still only samples of all possible grammatical sentences he will eventually utter. Knowledge of the language does not depend on formal instruction in grammar. Even if we knew all necessary grammatical rules, they would probably only confuse the child. He would probably ignore them.

The rules are learned by acquiring intuitions about the way words are represented in sentences. Interaction with the environment is paramount since it permits the child to sample sentence structures, try different sentences of his own, test alternatives, and obtain feedback on his decisions. Parents' responses to their children's utterances are the best training we know about so far. For example, when the child says the holophrase, "milk," the parent usually knows what the child means and the parent typically offers corrective feedback: "Oh, you spilled the milk on the floor!" or "Do you want some milk to drink?"

These kinds of reactions, elaborations, paraphrases, and corrections provide the child with the variety of experiences he needs to construct his own rules for sentences. From the primary linguistic inputs, the child can form hypotheses—that is, he can select from his store of grammars the one that matches or is appropriate to the data (Chomsky, 1965, pp. 32, 36). From what seem to be relatively haphazard conditions and in minimally acceptable language environments, the child accomplishes the remarkable feat of learning the grammatical rules. Even more remarkable, these rules will eventually enable him to understand and speak an infinite variety of grammatically correct sentences.

LANGUAGE, INFORMATION PROCESSING, AND COMPREHENSION

CONCEPT
LEARNING

The formation, identification, and use of concepts constitute significant features of thought. Concepts are categories of objects, ideas, or events that have some similar features in spite of other dissimilar features. For example, the butterfly, the ant, the bee, and the praying mantis are quite different from each other, yet their similarities lead us to group them as insects. Similarly, democracy, monarchy, socialism, and facism are distinct from each other, but they all have the common feature of being governments.

THE NATURE OF CONCEPTS

The class we put an object into depends on which of its features we focus on. If we classify by function, a wooden chair belongs with other pieces of furniture regardless of its construction material. If we classify by construction material, the chair belongs with other wooden objects regardless of its function.

With increasing experience, a person can clearly partition features of conceptual classes so that categories become precise and well differentiated. Minerals, for example, can be subdivided into metals or stones. Their frequency of occurrence can be subdivided into the categories of rare or common. All four features can then be used to form partitions that permit differentiation and cross-reference as well as formation of larger categories (see Figure 5-1). If you classified humans on the basis of sex (male and female) and age (child and adult) according to the format in Figure 5-1, you would put man, woman, boy, and girl into each category. Partitioning shows that concept formation requires more than merely learning attributes, features, or characteristics of objects; it shows that the learner must also learn rules for combining features and seeing the relationships among them.

CONCEPTS AND DISCIPLINES

Concepts help organize both our perceptions and our knowledge. Also, the nature of concepts varies from one discipline to another. Although all areas of study deal with the same real world, their differences reflect their

CAMROSE LUTHERAN COLLEGE
LIBRARY

different concepts of the world: for example, many disciplines study water, but the biologist considers its physiological functions; the chemist, its chemical composition; the physicist, its specific gravity; and the English teacher, its grammatical characteristics.

Minerals

	Metals	Stones	Classifications by rows
Rare	platinum silver gold	diamond sapphire emerald	all in this row are *rare*
Common	aluminum copper lead	limestone granite slate	all in this row are *common*
Classifica- tion by columns	all in this column are *metals*	all in this column are *stones*	all items in columns and rows are *minerals*

Frequency of Occurrence (vertical label on left)

Figure 5-1. An example of classification by partitioning features. (Adapted from Bower, G. H., et al. Hierarchical retrieval schemes in recall of categorized word lists. *Journal of Verbal Learning and Verbal Behavior*, 1969, **8**, 323-343. Copyright © 1969 by Academic Press, Inc. Used by permission.)

CONCEPT NAMES

Most classes of concepts have names or labels such as *rare metals, common stones, blonde girls, tall men,* and so on. Nevertheless, many concepts, clearly based on partitions of features, do not have names. For example, the set of terms *college, progress,* and *achievement* are different from the set of terms *punishment, danger,* and *war.* Aside from classifying the first group as *good* and the second as *bad,* it is difficult to distinguish these two categories further. Still, they can be partitioned by their rating on the semantic differential, which is a technique for rating words in terms of their good/bad, strong/weak, and active/passive meanings. The technique is described in more detail later. *College, progress,* and *achievement* are typically rated as positive on *evaluation* (good), *potency* (strong), and *activity* (active), while *punishment, danger,* and *war* are typically rated negative on *evaluation* but positive on *potency* and *activity.* Words such as *baby* and *bird* differ from these two categories since they have positive ratings on *evaluation* and *activity* but negative ratings on *potency.* Here is a summary of the examples:

	College	Punishment	Baby	House
Evaluation	+	−	+	+
Potency	+	+	−	+
Activity	+	+	+	−

CONCEPTS AND PERCEIVING

Concepts facilitate behavior. If you were to react to every stimulus as an independent event, you would be overwhelmed by the variety of stimuli. Obviously, however, you classify stimuli rather than treating each as an independent event. For example, the eye is capable of seeing more than a million color distinctions (including mixtures, hues, and saturations), but the differentiations we perceive to be significant fall into only a dozen or so categories that are represented by names of colors—although, if needed, we can make finer distinctions.

Concepts, then, pattern our experiences. Our experiences are abstracted, grouped, or regrouped into patterns, classes, hierarchies, and other structures. Learners also acquire and store information about how much variation is permissible for a newly experienced instance to be included in a certain category (Posner, 1969). Julesz (1974) shows that random search of disparate placements of dots leads to identification of patterns in stereoscopic perception. However, he indicates that this primitive search for patterns is later replaced by meaningful search based on knowledge of patterns. Even casual observation suggests that most of our concepts have been acquired without deliberate instruction.

CONCEPTS AND LEARNING

Aside from perceptually simplifying the environment, concepts are stored in memory as part of the cognitive structure. In the form of codes and rules, they allow us to interpret new situations without relearning the codes for each new experience. Concepts themselves can be mentally manipulated, combined, and related to one another to generate new ideas or principles without requiring direct observations or experiences. Consider such rules as "great demand for items in low supply results in increased selling price" or "an object is buoyed up to the extent of the weight of the water it displaces" in economics and physics, respectively. Such rules are very useful in problem solving. They are not generated directly from perceptual experience but result from concept manipulation in human minds. (Of course, such hypotheses are eventually verified or disproved by empirical data.) With appropriate concepts and principles, many problems can be worked out mentally, in a discussion, in writing, or on the drawing board without the errors that often accompany attempts to solve a problem without forethought.

CODING CONCEPTS

In the developmental process, cognition precedes the use of language. Once language has been developed, it maps, crystallizes, or codes experience into manageable form. An experiment by Heidbreder (1946; replicated by Di Vesta & Rickards, 1971) illustrates this sequence of events.

LABELS FOR EXPERIENCE: HEIDBREDER'S EXPERIMENT

Heidbreder's experiment consisted of 10 series of 12 pictures each (see Figure 5-2). The pictures were always different but represented concrete objects (animals, people), numerical quantities (two, five), or shapes (crossed sticks, circles). Using a general procedure known as reception learning, the experimenter showed the subject each picture from series I singly and in a random order and named it with an artificial word such as *ling, fard, mulp*, or *pran*. This was repeated with series II. For series III, IV, and V, the subject's task was to name each picture correctly before the experimenter did so.

The subject in these experiments was not told the definition of the artificial word that named each picture. He knew only that all pictures would be different and that he had to label them with one of the four words. By the time the last series was presented, most subjects could name each figure even though they had seen none of the figures before.

By looking at Figure 5-2, we see that an object called *ling* represents twoness; a *fard* is circular; a *pran* is a single object crossed by two others; and a *mulp* represents a tree. Subjects quickly learned which concept was shared by pictures with the same label. The concept also specified that there was a limited range of variation in the concept.

LABELS AND TRANSFER

Some evidence indicates that a verbal label attached to a new situation modifies the meaning of that situation and accordingly influences attitudes, learning, and transfer (Spiker, 1956). This view suggests that reactions to two different situations may be more similar if both are given the same

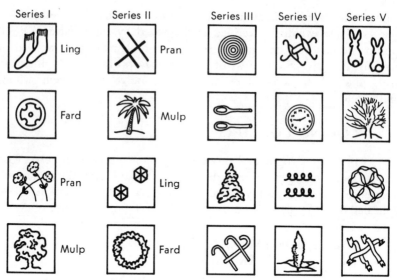

Figure 5-2. The materials and syllables used in Heidbreder's (1946) concept-formation task. The concepts are based on concrete objects, numerical quantities, and forms. After relating the syllables with the objects in series I and II, the reader should find it increasingly easier to name those in series III, IV, and V even though no object is repeated in any series. (Adapted from Heidbreder, E., The attainment of concepts: I. Terminology and methodology. *Journal of General Psychology,* 1946, **35,** 173–189. Reprinted by permission of The Journal Press.)

label—acquired equivalence of cues (AEC)—than if they are not. To illustrate, your initial meeting with two very different strangers might reasonably result in very different reactions to each stranger. But if you had been told that both strangers were strong liberals (or conservatives), your reaction to them would tend to be more similar. The label would have identified the strangers' common feature and would thus have influenced your behavior.

Also, events that are perceptually similar can be made distinctive by applying different labels—acquired distinctiveness of cues (ADC). Again, imagine meeting two persons. This time they are identical twins. Initially, you react only to their striking sameness but then a friend points out that one of the twins is a liberal and the other twin is a conservative. Now you may react to them quite differently. In addition to your reactions to their political views, you might perceive differences in their voices or physical features. The labels have provided a way to differentiate between them, and your behavior has changed accordingly. Acquired distinctiveness of cues thus provides a basis for increasing discrimination.

LABELS IN MOTOR LEARNING

Verbal labels can influence motor learning. In one laboratory study, subjects were to learn to move a rod from the center of a star into one of the points of the star on signal. The signal was one of five colored lights, which was flashed on a stimulus board placed in front of the subject. Different colors were flashed at different times. The subject's task was to identify which point of the star was to be associated with each color (McAllister, 1953). Before performing this task, some of the subjects received relevant pre-training. They learned to associate each color with an appropriate verbal label. For example, they may have associated *green* with *three o'clock, blue* with *six o'clock, purple* with *nine o'clock*, and so on. Then on the learning task, they were to learn to move the rod to the point of the star that corresponded to each color. However, they had to learn by practice and feedback only and were not told the relation between what they had learned on the verbal task and what they were to perform on the motor task. Each of three other groups received one of three kinds of irrelevant pre-training. Subjects learned such combinations as: *green-valiant* if they were in the relevant-stimulus/irrelevant-response group; *answer-three o'clock* if they were in the irrelevant-stimulus/relevant-response group; or *answer-valiant* if they were in the irrelevant-stimulus/irrelevant-response group. Then, each group performed the same learning tasks as did the relevant pre-training group. The relevant pre-training group outperformed the irrelevant pre-training groups: they learned more rapidly and made fewer errors.

In complex motor skills, verbal pre-training may correspond to labels, verbal codes, or elaborate verbal plans, all of which are potentially helpful in acquiring the skill. For example, when aircraft-pilot trainees were given a verbal plan for take-off, ascent, cruising, descent, and landing, the training time they required to solo was halved when compared to procedures that depend on practice only (Miller, Galanter, & Pribram, 1960). The verbal plan describes and lists in order of occurrence the movements and manipulations associated with desired maneuvers.

WHY DO LABELS MATTER?

Just how labels and verbal plans influence generalization and discrimination is controversial. Usually, labels appear to be potent instruments because their meanings transfer directly to the situation to which they are applied. The relationships are readily apparent. When we say, "Another boat is coming at us from the three o'clock position," the meaning is clear; we capitalize on relevant pre-training. The verbal label taps a relevant part of what we know, or our cognitive structure. However, in many laboratory studies, such as those with AEC and ADC, the labels are not inherently meaningful since they often are artificial words. Yet even applying the same artificial word to different situations facilitates generalization. Conversely, applying different artificial words facilitates discrimination among similar situations. Perhaps the mere fact of seeing different labels alerts the learner to look for differences in attributes, and upon seeing the same labels he looks for shared characteristics. Perhaps he reacts to the labels themselves: different labels enhance discrimination among differences in characteristics already there, while similar labels enhance generalization. Or, perhaps labels influence attention to configurations that can be shared with the labels: that is, some unique characteristic of the label—its sound, its written shape, its meaning, or some other feature—is associated with a similar characteristic of the situation. Although researchers do not agree on which explanation is correct, note that all of these explanations involve a degree of processing by the learner.

CONCEPT DEVELOPMENT

The formation of concepts appears to have relatively consistent characteristics at different stages of growth, though the stages are not as clearly identifiable as they are in the emergence of language.

COMPLEXES TO SUPERORDINATES

Initially, children's concepts seem to be in the form of partial concepts called complexes. A complex contains only some of the relevant features of the concept and tends to be less stable than a true concept. Vygotsky (1962, pp. 73–74) illustrates the complex by describing the evolution of the Russian word *sutki*, meaning day and night. Initially, this word meant a seam between two pieces of cloth that were sewn together. Then the word was used to describe any seam between two objects, such as the junction of two walls. Later it was extended, metaphorically, to mean the junction between night and day, or twilight, the time when day and night meet. Finally, it came to mean the time between one twilight and the next, or the 24-hour period called *sutki*. The chain of development of this word shows that each new link changed the meaning somewhat from the word's previous usage.

When the child initially learns to form concepts, he seems to use similar processes. If he is instructed to categorize blocks of different colors, sizes, and shapes, the very young child does not go directly to some superordinate category such as blue circles and then proceed to group all blue circles together. Instead, he may begin by categorizing three or four circles correctly but then he encounters a blue triangle; the triangle strikes his fancy, and he now begins to classify according to triangularity until some other attribute —perhaps brightness, some other color, or some other shape—attracts him. The very young child attempts to classify but the classes he uses are unstable.

Bruner and Olver (1963) explored the emergence of concepts from complexes in a series of studies. These researchers are interested in the way children grouped the objects rather than with the specific content of their groupings. Children in the first, fourth, and sixth grades were given lists of such terms as:

horn	radio
bell	book
telephone	newspaper

Then the child was asked how pairs of items in the list were alike:

horn-bell
bell-telephone
telephone-radio

Next, another item was added to the pairs and the child was again instructed to tell how the three terms were alike:

horn-bell-telephone
telephone-radio-book

As each set was completed, another item was added until all words in the list were included.

These investigators found that the use of superordinate categories increased directly with grade level. The sixth-grade children used nearly three times as many superordinates as did the first-grade children. Sixth-grade children said, "They are all means of communication," but younger children tended to use more complexes of various kinds: for example, when asked to classify "bell, telephone, and horn," fourth-grade children said "A telephone is like a bell because it has a bell in it; it is like a horn because you put your mouth up to a horn and you put your mouth up to a telephone."

The younger child's concepts are neither complete nor stable. Their initial classifications are based on perceptual features. It is as though young children were trying to find the rules the adult is using, but they are not quite certain which features are important. Nevertheless, the formation of complexes is a transitional phase toward developing rules for combining objects into more general, often abstract, superordinate categories. The use of complexes decreases as the child grows older, and there is a corresponding increase in the use of superordinates.

CONSERVATION OF CONCEPTS

Complex formation contradicts the popular notion that children overgeneralize. The evidence for overgeneralization is mostly anecdotal, being based on such observations as very young children calling any man "Daddy."

Saltz and his co-workers (1971) found that children tend to over-discriminate rather than overgeneralize. Six-year-old children were asked, "Is a father who goes to work, where he is a doctor, still a father?" Less than half of them said yes. On the other hand, more than three-fourths of the 8-year-olds said yes. Even more interesting were the responses of 8-year-olds to a similar question in which the father was depicted as a drunkard. These children believed that a father who becomes a drunkard is no longer a father. Saltz concludes that young children fail to conserve the concept because they see the dimensions as correlated: a father is good and a drunkard is bad; therefore a drunkard cannot be a father. In the first example, the children who fail to conserve the concept may reason that a man who has the role of father in the family is no longer a father when in his occupational role of doctor. Ervin and Foster (1960) also obtained similar evidence showing children's dependence on correlated traits: an object said to be large was also said to be strong. People who were said to be pretty were said to be happy and good. Such correlations of traits were found even up to the time children were 12 years old.

These findings are similar to rules formed in the pre-operational period, when children conclude that "bigger people are taller." Such a rule is valid up to a point but does not include all cases: adults who are bigger are not necessarily taller, doctors can be fathers, and not all people who are pretty are happy. This kind of reasoning is also similar to the reasoning that produces chain complexes. If *big, strong,* and *fast* are related in one's thinking, then the chain of reasoning may go from "Big things are strong" to "Strong things are fast." When *smiling, happy, pretty,* and *good* are correlated, the reasoning might go from "Smiling people are happy" to "Happy people are pretty" to "Pretty people are good." Without precise differentiations, there are fewer partitions; features are treated as equivalent, and the result is a potpourri with potential distinctions ignored. As these examples show, such concepts fail to differentiate aspects of the world in culturally useful ways.

AFFECTIVE AND EXPRESSIVE MEANING

There are several kinds of meanings. Denotative meanings of words are based on specific attributes such as those given in dictionary definitions. Other meanings of words consist of their more general connotations, usually with affective properties, such as good or bad. Still other meanings are implied by the way a word is used, by the way a sentence is phrased, by the choice of words, or by inflection. Such meanings are called expressive meanings. The meanings of the words we have been discussing up to this point in the chapter are denotative meanings shared by the language community. For example, the concept of all United States coins is an inclusive category. Any instance of the concept is round and has two sides. It has a picture, a date, and the word *liberty* on the front. On the other side is the value of the coin, a picture with symbolic value, the motto *E Pluribus Unum*, and the words, United States of America. The sub-categories of coins (penny, nickel, dime, quarter, half-dollar, and dollar) are clearly differentiated from one denomination to another. A coin collector may make even finer discriminations to identify specific qualities of coins or to identify a given coin in his collection. He may say that he has a proof, uncirculated, or mint-quality coin. These labels communicate features of his coins to other collectors.

The denotative meaning of categories consists of inclusive features (attributes that define what the concept is) and exclusive features (attributes that define what the concept is not). Such meanings are acquired by social reinforcement from other members of the language community—from parents, teachers, and peers. Through corrective feedback, the child comes to learn the differentiating features shared by the rest of the language community for all concepts.

CONNOTATIVE MEANINGS

Other kinds of meanings are more personalized than denotative meanings. These represent our feelings about the concepts in question. For example, while we can agree on the denotative meaning of the word *horse*, we may have a different affective meaning for this word. Affective meanings can be measured by using the semantic differential technique (Osgood, Suci, & Tannenbaum, 1957; Snider & Osgood, 1969), which is based on the assumptions that (1) connotative meanings can be represented by bipolar adjectives such as good/bad, active/passive, and strong/weak as affective features and (2) polarity is present to some degree in all referents. A number of rating scales constructed around bipolar adjectives are used for measuring connotative meaning. These scales may have as few as three or as many as 100 points, but ordinarily such scales have 7 points. The subject rates his meanings for a given word on these scales, as Figure 5-3 illustrates with one possible set of ratings for the word *horse*.

Much research has been conducted using the semantic-differential technique in cross-cultural studies (Miron & Osgood, 1966) and studies with children (Di Vesta & Walls, 1970). Results indicate that the semantic differential does not measure denotative meanings but provides an index of affective or connotative meaning—that is, the way a person feels about a concept. Try the technique yourself by rating a political event, a president, a friend, or a restaurant on all parts of the semantic differential in Figure 5-3.

Connotative meanings are personal. Compare your ratings of an event or person with the ratings made by another person who has a different outlook than you do. While we may all agree on the denotative meaning of, for example, representational art, some people consider it a good, powerful, and dynamic mode of expression while others consider it bad, dull, and static. Statistical analyses of the ratings of thousands of subjects on hundreds of concepts consistently identify three dimensions of connotative meanings: evaluation (as measured by the good-bad and similar scales), potency (strong-weak), and activity (active-passive). Although the semantic differential is intended to tap idiosyncratic meanings (meanings specific to a given person), shared experience with any concept in a given language community tends to make affective meanings similar also. Accordingly, the technique is often used to identify differences among groups.

EXPRESSIVE MEANINGS

Brown (1965) has described a kind of meaning that he calls *expressive*; it is similar to connotative meaning since it conveys affect, or feelings, but instead of being measured directly, expressive meaning is inferred from the words another person uses to convey his idea, together with his accompanying intonation patterns, physical gestures, or postures. Although there is little data about this kind of meaning, clearly much speech implies feelings beyond what is conveyed by the words themselves.

Brown illustrates expressive meaning by describing a conversation (Brown, 1965, pp. 330–332). During a dinner party, a political scientist and an economist are discussing the economic development of Nigeria, and the economist says, "That's a place I've not been to." The political scientist immediately replies, "I've not been there either, and it isn't the only place I haven't been to." The immediate consequence of this brief interchange is embarrassment to the hostess and anger (socially controlled, however) on the part of the economist. Later, the political scientist is overly polite to the

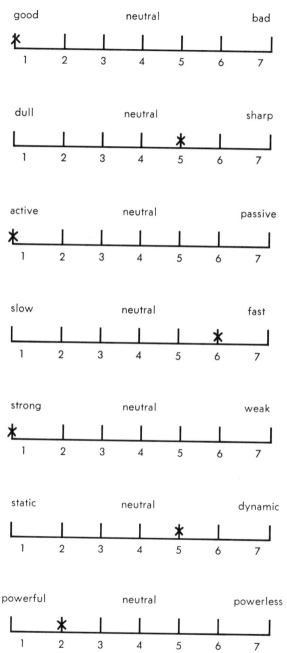

Figure 5-3. An example of one person's semantic differential ratings for the word *horse*. The x shows the rater's response on each scale.

economist and, Brown says, "... everyone knew why." Note that the connection between the two comments is not explicit yet the underlying connotation is clear to all.

Brown's analysis of this interchange indicates that the economist made the remark as a result of certain forces. First, he wanted to state that he had not traveled to Nigeria, which he might have accomplished by simply saying, "I've never been there." Second, he wanted to indicate that he was not totally inexperienced—in fact, that he had quite a bit of experience. He could have said, "I've been everywhere but to Nigeria," but that would be bragging. Third, in such situations, custom dictates that one should avoid bragging. The economist's actual comment was the result of all three forces. The political scientist grasped the three forces that prompted the economist's remark and the political scientist's reply was meant to embarrass the economist for his attempt to brag.

Speakers construct sentences to convey both denotative meanings and connotative meanings through prosodic features: stress on certain words, pauses, changing loudness, changing tempo, changing pitch, changing intonation patterns, or accents. (These characteristics parallel similar characteristics that account for expression in music.) Consider the effect of stress or accent on each of the marked words in the following sentences by reading each sentence aloud and emphasizing the indicated words:

> I hope you will walk right home from school.
> I hope you will walk right home from school.
> I hope you will walk right home from school.
> I hope you will walk right home from school.
> I hope you will walk right home from school.
> I hope you will walk right home from school.
> I hope you will walk right home from school.

Undoubtedly you were able to produce, through variations in stress, a different meaning for each sentence. In each sentence, you may have been able to indicate the main feature you were emphasizing. Each sentence might be changed further by adding gestures such as pointing, smiling, shaking a finger to threaten punishment, and scowling or bodily movements such as folding one's arms, running after a child, or holding a child affectionately. It is amazing how many variations of this surface structure are possible by changing prosodic features and contextual cues.

People are sensitive to expressive communication. Our speech, manner, or dress can give us away when we say one thing and mean another. Although methods for expressive communication may vary, they are consistent enough within a language community so that expressive meanings can be interpreted and differentiated at least into hostility, aggression, ingratiation, politeness, overbearingness, and submissiveness.

Our understandings of connotative and expressive meanings suggest the complexity of the conceptual system. In addition, since expressive content is shared by the language community, it does influence and control the behavior of others. With one stress pattern, a teacher's statement might function as a positive verbal reinforcer. With only slight changes in expression, it might function as punishment. Parents and teachers often inadvertently use affective undertones, which may become associated with the situational context and may promote development of approach-avoidance behaviors in children; undertones of approval may lead to a warm, supportive classroom climate; and hostile, sarcastic undertones may lead to a cold climate that encourages alienation. As with other learning, the effects of expressive content may generalize from a specific situation (a classroom with a specific teacher) to other, similar situations (to all classrooms).

SOME GENERAL CONDITIONS OF CONCEPT LEARNING

Concepts are learned by corrective feedback. Learners experience examples of a concept in several settings and try to identify the common features of the examples. Then, by feedback (generally from an external source such as a teacher or parent), they learn whether a given example is or is not an example of the concept. Learners identify both the important characteristics that define the concept and the rule for combining these features.

REDUNDANCY

Some concepts consist of only one feature. Other concepts consist of redundant features—that is, when one feature occurs, other features always accompany it. If we assume that whenever a crawling creature has three body segments it also always has six legs and two wings, then these characteristics are redundant; whenever one is present the others are also present. Concepts with many redundant features are more easily learned than concepts with few redundant features. In learning to classify such objects, the learner sees them as a configuration of all attributes. Eventually, one predicts the remaining attributes by seeing only one or two. In fact, the filling-in process is characteristic of well-learned concepts.

Assume that color, size, and shape are irrelevant attributes for classifying our crawling creatures. The concept-learning task becomes more difficult as the number of irrelevant features relative to the relevant features increases because the learner has more difficulty in sorting out defining characteristics from non-defining ones. Therefore, teachers often use line drawings or similar abstractions to identify the important features of a concept. For example, the circulatory system would be difficult to identify in the body itself because surrounding tissues obscure it. Initial experience with line drawings shows the important locations of the blood vessels and highlights what the student is to look for so that later identification in more complex settings will be easier. Line drawings provide a wholistic view of the circulatory system as a system, which would be difficult without initial abstraction.

FEEDBACK AND
POSITIVE AND NEGATIVE INSTANCES

In practical situations as well as in the learning laboratory, the student is helped to identify concept features by being shown positive instances (examples in which the concept features are present) and negative instances (which consist of examples with no defining features or partly defining features). If the subject is to acquire the concept of large white squares, any large white square would be a positive instance. A correct identification would lead to positive feedback. If he selected a small white square, a large black square, or a large white triangle (all of which are negative instances), he would receive negative feedback. A series of positive and negative instances are correlated with positive (when he is correct) or negative (when he is wrong) feedback.

With feedback, the learner can compare and contrast positive and negative instances. Observers cannot know that the subject understands the concept until he responds correctly to negative instances; the pupil must be given an opportunity to identify negative instances. If the student is shown the lymphatic system and calls it the blood circulatory system, he clearly has not identified the blood system by its correct attributes. Similarly, if a pupil calls something that has two body segments and eight legs an insect, he has failed to use the correct attributes of insects in making his identification, since insects have three body segments and six legs. Nor does one really know whether a pupil can read the word *John*, even though he can select it correctly from among such other words as *John, Elephant, The*, or *Zebra*. Discrimination tasks that require precise differentiations—such as selecting the word *John* from among *Joseph, Join, Jim*, or *Jolly*—will help the pupil focus on the critical features that distinguish these words. Correct performance of these tasks will also convince the observer that the subject understands the concept. Concept learning requires learning what the concept is not as well as what it is. Precise comparison of positive and negative instances is essential for the identification of critical features.

RULES FOR COMBINING
CONCEPT FEATURES

In all concept learning, the learner must learn not only the defining features but also the way these features are combined. Some are combined in simple conjunctive relations of two or more attributes—such as the combination of stars and stripes together with their number, color, and positioning that makes up our concept of the American flag. If an example contains only one of these features, it is not an instance of the concept. Concepts based on simple combinations of two or more features are called *conjunctive* concepts. Other concepts require learning a rule that relates the two features in an either/or relationship. It can be one or the other but not both. For example, a strike is called in baseball when the ball goes over the plate at a certain height or when the batter swings at the ball and misses it. Such concepts are called *disjunctive* concepts. Other concepts, especially abstract ones, are based on rules that combine conjunctive and disjunctive relationships.

FINDING ATTRIBUTES VERSUS
FINDING RULES

Most experiments in concept learning have required learners to identify both the features and the rules for combining the features. Bourne (1967) attempted to separate the effects of the two kinds of learning. He asked, "What effect does knowing a rule have when the learner forms a concept? . . . Is there a difference, in concept acquisition, between learners who know the rule and must identify the attributes compared to the learner who knows the attributes but must identify the rule?"

In conducting experiments designed to answer these questions, Bourne and his colleagues administered a series of problems that required subjects to identify the presence or absence of two features such as color (green and non-green) or shape (square or non-square). Different features were used in each problem, and a different rule had to be used to determine the concept in each problem. Half of the subjects in the experiment were given the rule; thus, they had only to learn the attributes and how to apply the rule. The other half were given the attributes; thus they had only to learn the rule and how to apply it.

Figure 5-4 shows the results of this study. In answer to his question, Bourne found that identifying the rule (when attributes are known) is easier than identifying the attributes (when the rule is known). Second, the order of difficulty in using the different kinds of rules remains essentially the same whether the learner has to identify the rule or the attributes. Third, the differences in difficulty are apparent only in the initial problems. With successive practice, differences disappeared. Apparently subjects learned how to learn.

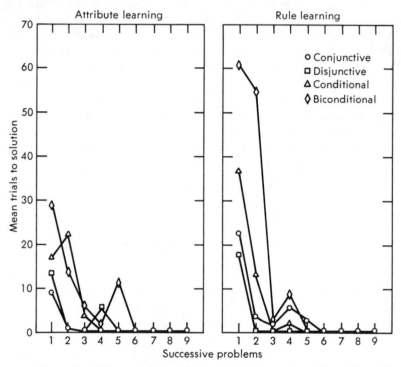

Figure 5–4. Mean trials to solution of rule learning and attribute identification problems based on 4 different rules. (From Bourne, L. E., Jr. Learning and utilization of conceptual rules. In B. Kleinmuntz [Ed.], *Concepts and the Structure of Memory.* Copyright © 1967 by John Wiley & Sons, Inc. Reprinted by permission.)

The concepts used in laboratory settings seem complex but are probably much less complex than the concepts learned in school. The optimistic conclusion of Bourne's experiments is that, given sufficient practice in concept formation, processing difficulties can be overcome. The curriculum should provide practice in process learning. The pupil can be instructed to perceive relevant attributes, combine attributes, and use information from negative instances. There is little reliable information on how such instruction should be implemented. However, if we extrapolate from our knowledge about language learning, direct instruction may be less important than systematic exposure to a variety of concept-formation tasks. The teacher could provide examples of the concept in different contexts. He could show line drawings that emphasize important features of the concept. He could offer opportunities for the pupil to respond to both positive and negative instances. Finally, he could provide the pupil with corrective feedback. From many such experiences with concepts based on increasingly difficult rules, this discovery or inquiry method of teaching will help the student learn the processes involved in concept formation.

CHAPTER
SIX
LANGUAGE, MEANING, AND COMPREHENSION

At the turn of the century, Ebbinghaus (1885) invented the nonsense syllable in an attempt to study learning and remembering in its raw form. He recognized that meaning was an influential variable in forming associations and in relating learning material to what was already known by the learner. Any research using common words would not be studying new learning; instead, it would involve the transfer of earlier learning to facilitate or hinder the learning of new materials. The nonsense syllable was intended to circumvent these problems since it presumably had no meaning.

Over the years, nonsense syllables have enjoyed tremendous popularity in studies of paired-associate learning, serial learning, remembering, forgetting, and even as signals in motor learning. Yet, meaning could not be eliminated; learners made nonsense syllables meaningful despite the experimenter's intentions. For example, a learner required to learn the pair *bik-rok* might translate it into *big rock*, or he might use the third letter, *k*, of each syllable as a cue for forming associations. Experimenters have attempted to control these processes. For example, they have tried using trigrams (three-letter nonsense words) composed only of consonants, such as *lfx, hlc,* or *qwk,* to substitute for nonsense syllables in the hope that it would be more difficult to attach meaning to them than to nonsense syllables. But consonant trigrams do not avoid the problem; *lfx* might become "I'll have eggs"; *hlc* might be translated to an acronym for Home Loan Corporation; and *qwk* might be considered an abbreviation of "quick." The problem is complicated by society's prevalent use of acronyms.

Such research problems show that the learner is busily engaged while learning and that he contributes intellectual materials and learning tools to the learning task. The learning materials are one's personal knowledge and one's preparation for the task at hand. The tools are strategies for processing the information. When one strategy becomes preferred, used more frequently, or used to the exclusion of others, we speak of a *cognitive style*, which is the learner's characteristic way of relating his abilities or knowledge to what is to be learned.

THE LEARNER'S COGNITIVE STRUCTURE
AND TASK REQUIREMENTS

By the learner's cognitive structure, we mean what the learner knows—what he has learned through verbal and non-verbal experience. Achievement tests attempt to measure cognitive structure but they are inadequate since they measure only knowledge of facts or, at best, concepts. The cognitive structure is more than a collection of experiences—it also includes the way one organizes one's experiences, which differs among individuals. Most of our understanding of cognitive structure is theoretical and is the result of inferences from experiments on learning and memory; new learning seems to depend largely on how past learning has been organized. Figure 6–1 shows one attempt to define a cognitive structure.

Organized knowledge is differentiated into clear categories that are structured and subdivided further. No known achievement test taps these very important characteristics of the cognitive structure.

MODIFYING THE MEANING OF
A CONCEPT

The learning task can be manipulated by the teacher to parallel the characteristics of the learner's cognitive structure, which can facilitate learning. Language features such as pronounciability, familiarity, frequency, associative strength, connotative meaning, concreteness, word imagery, and other stimuli can contribute to the efficiency of learning.

Meaning of a word. An important variable involved in learning is meaning. Saltz (1971) observes that the meaning of a word (or a sentence) is the set of things to which the word (or sentence) refers. If two words are seen to be associated, it is because they refer to something in common. Whether an individual associates two words depends on his cognitive structure—that is, whether his organization of experience relates these two words in any way. To enhance communication, the meaning of an event for a given person should correspond to definitions agreed on through common usage by all members of a language community.

Meaningfulness. In contrast to meaning, meaningfulness is the extent to which a word or sentence has meaning. Loosely interpreted, meaningfulness depends on the number of different associations a word has in typical usage as well as the stability of the associations in a variety of contexts. Saltz (1971) describes these characteristics of meaningfulness as "(a) the tendency for the word to conserve prior meanings ... (b) the differentiation of the word ... (c) the level of abstractness or amount of

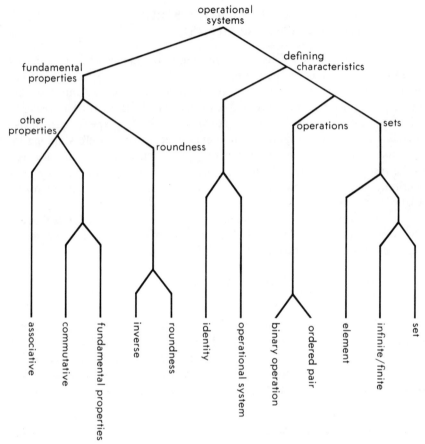

Figure 6-1. An example of the hierarchical arrangement (cognitive structure) of key concepts of operational systems based on word-association measures. (From Shavelson, R. J. Methods for examining representations of a science subject-matter structure in a student's memory. *Journal of Research in Science Teaching*, 1973. Reprinted by permission of the National Association for Research in Science Teaching.)

imagery evoked by the word (which appears to be related to the specificity of the word in the cognitive space)" (Saltz, 1971, p. 340).

Associative meanings and meaningfulness affect (a) the modification of an existing concept and (b) the way a word or concept affects new learning. An existing concept will resist subsequent modification if it has been frequently experienced. Frequency and familiarity tend to make an existing meaning more stable. A concept with only one meaning will be more stable and therefore more resistant to change than one with many meanings, frequency being equal. A word with one meaning is used the same way each time. If a word has more than one meaning, it is more flexible but also less stable. Therefore, the meaning of a highly differentiated concept (one with many different meanings) can be modified more easily than a concept with a single meaning since new meanings can be placed into any number of compartments in the cognitive structure. A concept with only a single meaning allows for new meaning to be placed in only one part of the cognitive structure, which hinders acquisition of new meanings. On the other hand, a concept will acquire new meanings more easily to the extent that it has been experienced in many contexts.

RELATING CONCEPTS TO OTHER CONCEPTS

As words or concepts are used in new learning tasks, they are placed into new relationships to each other, such as paired-associate learning, serial learning, or connected discourse.

The variables that were listed earlier as contributing to the efficiency of learning (meaning, meaningfulness, pronounceability, familiarity, and imagery) also facilitate the linkage of concepts. Imagery variables tend to be most influential when they are varied on the stimulus side of a paired-associate task. Stimuli with high imagery tend to be quickly identified and clarified by the learner. Stimuli that have less vivid imagery require familiarization before they become useful cues. Accordingly, learners use vivid stimuli more efficiently than dull stimuli.

In contrast to imagery, meaningfulness is most influential when varied on the response side of the paired-associate task. Responses in paired-associate learning must be linked with the stimuli. The more associates the response has, the easier it will be for the learner to find some relationship between one of these associates and the stimuli. A cue that has only a single associate (a cue that is low on the dimension of meaningfulness) requires a period of time for the subject to identify the link. Responses that are low in meaningfulness tend to interrupt the learner's efficiency.

STRATEGIES FOR COMPREHENDING

How are the cognitive structure and the requirements of the task matched to facilitate learning and retrieval? The answer is far from being understood, although the intensity of investigation in this area reflects great concern.

Intention.   Clearly, intention is important. If I hold a pencil up in front of a class and say, "I shall ask you the color of this pencil at the end of the term," most of the class will remember the color. Or, if I say, "I shall ask you to recall the pair *potato-frog* at the end of the semester," most students will remember the pair; in fact, three out of four students I asked a year later remembered the pair of terms without further cues.

People sometimes remember trivia while they forget things that are considered more important. This occurs for several reasons: (a) the trivia is clearly differentiated from other material presented at the same time—it attracts attention and is distinguished from its context; (b) it is labeled by the learner as something to be remembered; and (c) the learner carefully identifies ways of storing the trivia so as to make it easily retrievable. The facilitating influence of these factors shows up especially when the learner is allowed ample time for learning. About 7 to 10 seconds of concentration following presentation of a pair seems to suffice for optimal learning. During this time, called the practice period, learners do more than merely repeat the material; they use strategies to code the materials into a form that will allow for easy retrieval later. While there are many such strategies, the following discussion will cover strategies that relate to language learning and use.

ASSOCIATIVE STRATEGIES

A study by Martin, Boersma, and Cox (1965) demonstrated how learners engage in learning. The subjects learned several pairs of two-syllable nonsense words (*meardon-zumap, bodkin-nostaw, tarop-gojey*). After learning the list, each pair was again shown and the subjects were asked how they had learned it. Seven major strategies, ranging from no strategy to relatively complex transformations, were identified. As Table 6-1 shows, only a few students approached the task as a rote-learning problem. In addition, the number of correct responses was directly related to the complexity of the strategy used; that is, the more active the strategy, the more efficient the learning.

MEDIATIONAL STRATEGIES

Verbal mediation is related to associative strategies. As words are experienced in various contexts, they acquire new associations and meanings that can then influence new learning.

The RAT.   Mediational ability is illustrated by Mednick and Mednick's (1967) Remote Associates Test (RAT). This test presented triplets of

Table 6-1. Classification of associative strategies.

Category level	Type of cue subject reported using	Example of verbal report
1. No reported associations (12%)	S was not able to state how he managed to make the association.	*Sagrole-polef*: "Don't know how I learned this pair."
2. Repetition (11%)	S reported rehearsing the pair.	*Volvap-nares*: "Just kept repeating these words to myself."
3. Single letter cues (14%)	S reported using a single letter in each of the paralogs in making the association.	*Tarop-Gojey*: "Noticed that each word contained an *o*."
4. Multiple letter cues (10%)	S reported using multiple letters in each of the paralogs.	*Sagrole-polef*: "Each word contains an *ole*."
5. Word formation (6%)	S reported that an actual word was embedded in one or both of the paralogs and made use of these words in making the association.	*Meardon-zumap*: "The word *ear* is contained in meardon and learned that *ear* goes with zumap."
6. Superordinate (29%)	S reported selecting elements from each of the two paralogs that had some relationship to each other.	*Sagrole-polef:* "Sagrole begins with *s* and *polef* with *p*: thought of State Police"
7. Syntactical (18%)	S reported selecting elements from each of the two paralogs and embedding these elements into a sentence, phrase, or clause.	*Rennet-quipson:* "Changed *rennet* to *Bennet* and saw *quips* in *quipson*—thought: Bennet Cerf quips on TV."

From Martin, C. J., Boersma, F. J., & Cox, D. L. A classification of associative strategies in paired-associate learning. *Psychonomic Science*, 1965, **3**, 455–456. Reprinted by permission.

real words for which the respondent was to find a word common to all three. For example, the words *rat-blue-moon* might be linked by the word *cheese* (rats eat cheese, blue cheese, the moon is made of cheese). In this example, *cheese* is the mediator.

Joe learns a mediator; Bill does not. Mediational links can be manipulated experimentally in the laboratory by a number of different procedures. A common procedure has become known as the *A-B, B-C, A-C* design. This design can be illustrated by substituting artificial words for the letter symbols. Imagine that a learner, called Joe, first learns a list of such pairs as *volvap-nares* (call this *A-B*). After the list has been thoroughly learned, he learns another list of such pairs as *nares-brugen* (call this *B-C*). Note that in this pair, *nares* is now the stimulus, while in the previous list it was the response. When the second list has been learned thoroughly, the learner learns a third list of pairs such as *volvap-brugen* (call this *A-C*). Now imagine that a second learner, Bill, engages in the same tasks except his second list consists of such pairs as *goken-brugen* (call this *X-C*).

Joe and Bill learn the first two lists in about the same amount of time. (We are assuming that Joe and Bill have equal learning ability.) However, Joe learned the third list more quickly than Bill. Recall that Joe's lists linked *volvap* and *brugen*, so for Joe, *nares* became an implicit response to *volvap* (learned in the *A-B* phase) and a stimulus for *brugen* (learned in the *B-C* phase). Joe had a mediator, and Bill did not.

The mediation process is outlined in Figure 6–2.

	Joe	Bill
	(Learned a mediator)	(Did not learn a mediator)
Phase 1	Learns *A-B* (*volvap-nares*)	Learns *A-B* (*volvap-nares*)
Phase 2	Learns *B-C* (*nares-brugen*)	Learns *X-C* (*goken-brugen*)
Phase 3	Learns *A-C* (*volvap-brugen*)	Learns *A-C* (*volvap-brugen*)
	$A \to (r_B \to s_B) \to C$	$A \to (r_B \to x) \to C$
	Facilitation	No Facilitation

Figure 6–2. An example of the mediation process.

Experiments such as this show that mediation, especially in paired-associate learning, is important in linking two items together. Interestingly, the mediator facilitates learning of the *A-C* pairs even though *A* and *C* were not, themselves, linked. They are related in the learner's mind through his processing of the information.

CUES TO MEANING

While mediation processes hint at how information is processed, absorbing the meaning of a sentence requires the learner to understand the sentence. Grammar clarifies the meaning of a sentence as well as the meaning of specific words in the sentence. More important the interaction between a word and its grammatical role indicates meaning. Thus, with two like "The play was a *hit*," and "The boy *hit* the ball," the agent-action-object relationships tell us which meaning of *hit* to use in each case.

IDENTIFYING MEANING FROM FEATURES

To identify meaning, the reader/listener depends on several categories of his knowledge of words and words in sentences, as Figure 6-3 shows. At one level, syntactic markers indicate how a word can be used grammatically. *Bachelor*, for example, is marked as a noun. At another level, words can be marked in terms of general semantic features, such as human or animal, male or female, young or old. However, to tell how the word is used in a sentence, further distinctions are required. These indicate exactly how one meaning is different from another. The many meanings of *bachelor*, then, can be isolated to make sense out of what might otherwise seem ambiguous sentences.

Consider the following sentences:

The knight honored his bachelor's bravery.
The bachelor bought a gift for his fiancée.
The bachelor was photographed after graduation.
The bachelor slid from the ice into the water when the hunters came.

Now look at Figure 6-3 and return to these sentences. After the meanings of bachelor are clarified by Figure 6-3, the sentences are no longer ambiguous.

CONTEXT SENSITIVITY

Much of one's interpretation of a word or phrase in a sentence depends on the reader/listener's idea of the writer/speaker's intent. Sometimes, graphic features are less important than the context in which they appear. Consider the symbols **13** and **boss** in these sentences:

13ake a cake for the party.
The cards were *em bossed.*
Is **13** an unlucky number?
There were **boss** people.

In the first two sentences, the symbols appear as letters; in the second two sentences, they appear as numbers. Intent, as indicated by the context, is more influential in interpreting these symbols than mechanical decoding processes.

Children delight in playing word games that exploit the effect of context on changing the meaning of a phonological combination. See how

Figure 6-3. A hierarchical arrangement of meaning assigned to the word *bachelor.* (From Katz, J. J., & Fodor, J. A. The structure of a semantic theory. *Language,* 1963, **39**, 170–210. Reprinted by permission of the Linguistic Society of America.)

the meaning of the sounds represented in /eye-scream/ changes in the context of the familiar children's jingle,

/*Eye-scream*/, you scream, we all scream for /*eye-scream*/.

Context becomes important in many aspects of reading. Familiarity with the language, the author's writing style, and the subject matter enable the reader to depend as much on context for interpretation as on specific words. A common test of which features of a word are used to identify it uses mutilated words such as .ʌꝑꝑ!ɔ. Even a badly disfigured word can be read in context as in

John hit the bal'.

Furthermore, we don't even need every letter of a word to read a sentence. You can still understand this sentence

ev_n w_th _ve_y t_ir_ le_te_ ta_en _ut.

The writing style we use for telegrams also shows that entire words can be omitted with little loss of meaning, as in the following message:

Read book. Test Friday.

This certainly conveys as much meaning as "Read the book because a test has been scheduled for Friday." The sentence provides additional information, which is unnecessary. However, for sentences taken out of context or for readers with little related information, the additional information in the sentence does facilitate understanding. In each of these examples, the deletions made interpretation a little more difficult, but restoring all letters and words to their proper places makes these examples equally understandable to both experienced and inexperienced readers.

SOME SOURCES OF INFORMATION IN READING

The reader/listener brings as much to communication as does the written or spoken signal (for example, see Smith, 1971). He may supply words he didn't hear or anticipate words not yet spoken or read. Fill in the appropriate word in this sentence: "The teacher asked the pupil to give the an_____." Note that you immediately eliminate some possibilities. Certain constraints help you select the correct word.

Spelling rules.   Certain letters are precluded since *an* in a morpheme is rarely followed by such consonants as h, f, r, or w.

Syntactic rules.   Articles such as *the* are not typically followed by other articles, verbs, or conjunctions in the English language. Accordingly, the word in our example is most likely a noun, thereby eliminating such words as *anonymous* or *anechoic.*

Semantic rules.   While *anchor, animal, anteater, andromeda,* or *anarchy* might be used, they do not make sense in the context of the sentence although they may be grammatically correct. However, *answer* or *antonym* would meet both constraints, although *answer* is most likely.

Relational rules. Selection restrictions affect which word could fill the blank in the sentence, "The _____ asked the pupil to give the answer." Here, agent-action-object relations are important. Typically, such sentences require the agent to be a noun with animate or human features, such as *teacher, parent,* or *man.* In the sentence "I counted the b_____," we might use *boys* but not *boy.* Furthermore, in some cases reversibility between the subject and object suggests which word can be used. Thus, we could say "The truck hit the curb" but not "The curb hit the truck"; in this case, the subject and object are irreversible. However, had *boy* and *ball* been used in the same sentence, they would be reversible since they could be interchanged meaningfully.

MEANING, WORDS, AND REFERENCE

Anomaly, ambiguity, and paraphrase are sometimes based on syntactical considerations. Katz and Fodor (1963) discuss the sentence, "The stuff is light"; *light* has two meanings, either color or weight, thereby making the sentence ambiguous. Its meaning could be clarified by rewriting the sentence to "The stuff is light enough to carry." Syntax now identifies the meaning, since *carry* applies to weight but not color.

Context again. Context is important for identifying specific aspects of a word's meaning. To a naive learner, the word *square* may be ambiguous. Paired with a triangle, the square's four-sided character is emphasized. Paired with a circle, its straight-edged character is emphasized. If the square is simultaneously presented with a circle, a triangle, and an oblong rectangle its characteristics of being straight-edged, four-sided, and having sides of equal length are emphasized. Most words have several aspects that the listener/reader must differentiate.

Helping the reader/listener. The speaker elaborates his meaning to the extent he feels he must help the listener differentiate among alternatives. The speaker does not have to help the listener choose from among all possible alternatives since both speaker and listener rely on context and experience.

Meaning is relative. Any word or idea conveys a set of alternative meanings. Many alternatives mean more information but also more ambiguity. Accordingly, syntactical arrangements, contrasts, and contexts clarify meaning, thereby reducing the alternative features to the one to which the listener/reader must attend. A characteristic of a good reader is the ability to use this information efficiently in arriving at the correct meaning of the word.

On being informed.   The more knowledge one has, the more words are available to him for communication. The fluent speaker with a large vocabulary can specify what he means more exactly than the less gifted speaker. As a listener, the more informed person will have a more finely divided cognitive structure; accordingly, he will be able to identify the speaker's intentions through minimal contextual cues.

CHAPTER
SEVEN
LANGUAGE,
ORGANIZATION OF INFORMATION,
AND RETRIEVAL IN MEMORY

Ebbinghaus' (1885) classic research on forgetting was the beginning of many studies on learning and retention. Ebbinghaus used the copy notion of retention: good recall was exact recall, which was influenced by practice, time spent in study, stimulus characteristics, response characteristics, and relationships between stimuli and responses in paired-associate or serial learning tasks.

Other explanations of memory have occurred from time to time since Ebbinghaus' work. Freud's notion of repression in psychoanalytic theory emphasized motivational influences—that is, unpleasant events were repressed more readily than pleasant events. Bartlett's (1932) monumental work on remembering described the reconstructive processes in recall of information. Gestaltists emphasized change or reorganization of the memory trace early in the retention interval. More recently, the permanence of memory has been associated with ribonucleic acid (RNA), which might be the physiological basis for synthesis, encoding, or mediation of memory (Hydén, 1969).

TWO PROCESSES OF MEMORY

Memory is a complex process. No single explanation explains it adequately. Peterson and Peterson (1959) examined the possibility that short-term memory (STM) is distinct from long-term memory (LTM). Information remains in STM for a short while (a few seconds at most) and is subject to rapid displacement. You may have experienced this effect by finding a phone number in the directory only to forget it before you had a chance to dial or by being introduced to a person only to forget that person's name a few seconds later. Information can be held in STM by rehearsal. If it is coded (linked to the cognitive structure) in meaningful form, it is transferred to LTM, where it is held for longer periods of time, probably permanently. However, this rarely happens with telephone numbers.

Meaningfully learned information is stored in coded fashion—probably in hierarchically organized compartments that are much like a filing system of categorical information—rather than as a hodgepodge of isolated individual items. When it is retrieved, material is also affected by central thought processes that structure and organize the material. Thus, structure, organization, coding, and grouping influence both storage and retrieval.

Chapter Seven illustrates some effects of organization on retrieval mechanisms. The learner is viewed as an active organism that codes new information into a form that is meaningful.

EPISODIC AND SEMANTIC MEMORY

Tulving (1972) recently made an outstanding analysis of episodic and semantic memory, which is briefly summarized here.* *Episodic memory* is the recall of isolated, discrete events, usually personal or autobiographical, that are learned as independent episodes. For example, you may remember which day of the week July 4th fell on last year; you may recall that in a verbal learning experiment in which you participated, the nonsense syllable *lom* was the stimulus for the response *house*; or you may remember that the person you met at the Jones' house was John Doe. You recall these examples in terms of their relationship to some aspect of time, to some specific place. You may even be able to reconstruct where you were and what you were doing at 5:00 PM a year ago by relating such events.

Semantic memory, on the other hand, consists of meaningful information. For example, you know that the capitol of the United States is Washington, D.C.; you can describe the discovery of vulcanization of rubber; you know the numerical equivalent of π and that it occurs in formulas for finding the area and circumference of a circle. These examples are clearly remembered because they are integrated with other conceptual categories rather than being unique events; they are coded experiences that are meaningful for reasons other than the time at which they occurred.

The distinctions in cognitive functions between these two kinds of memory can now be elaborated further. In many ways, episodic and semantic memory correspond to differences in arbitrary learning and meaningful learning, respectively, as suggested by Ausubel (1968).

EPISODIC MEMORY

Episodic memory is a faithful record of experiences, which are generally stored by the learner in an arbitrary way. Experiences are associated with a period of time or simultaneously experienced events, but they

---

* Adapted from Tulving, E., Episodic and semantic memory. In E. Tulving & W. Donaldson (Eds.), *Organization of memory*. Copyright © 1972 by Academic Press, Inc. Used by permission.

remain isolated from other aspects of what the individual knows on a conceptual level—that is, they remain isolated from the cognitive structure. In fact, no other association besides the occurrence of the event is required for it to be registered, stored, or retrieved. All that is needed to prompt recall are such questions as "When did the event happen?" or "Where did it happen?" The subject then remembers such features as "It was a hot day," "There was a flash of light," "The person was tall and walking fast," or "I learned a list of eight nonsense-syllable pairs at 2:00 PM, including *buf* and *zug*." Recall of such episodes is usually in somewhat the same detail as it was initially perceived. Thus, it sometimes is called *reproductive memory*. Unlike semantic memory, which can be retrieved in different ways than it was initially experienced, episodic memory can be recalled only in the form in which it was stored earlier.

SEMANTIC MEMORY

If you were learning English as a foreign language and heard or saw the word *put* you might place it with *pat, pit, pot*, or *pet* because it shares acoustical and graphemic similarities. Such a grouping is based on primary characteristics—perceptual features, in this case. However, a somewhat different process might be used in learning valences of elements. If you already know the valence and other common characteristics of iodine, fluorine, and chlorine, when you learn about bromine—another member of the family of elements called halogens—you can generate its characteristics; it comes to occupy a corresponding position in the cognitive structure with other members of the halogens because of its underlying meaning. Semantic memory is characterized by relating the meanings of ideas.

Semantic memory encodes and assimilates new information to what is already known. The specific input event is superceded by its more general conceptual form. It is bromine's properties that allow it to be grouped with halogens, not the fact that someone conducted a demonstration with bromine the day before or that bromine is a certain color. Yavuz and Bousfield (1959) conducted an experiment that demonstrates a similar phenomenon. Subjects learned a list of foreign words, each of which was associated with another word implying a pleasant (home, reward, vacation) or unpleasant (punishment, danger, poison) feeling. Later, subjects could not recall the English equivalents of the foreign words but could recall the general tone of the words.

When information reaches semantic memory, it is related to other information that may have been learned much earlier. For example, the student who learns about bromine today can easily relate this concept to what he learned a year ago about the halogen family. Similarly, when one reads a story, it may first enter episodic memory but its ideas are then translated into a general theme that is stored in semantic memory. Information in semantic memory takes such general forms as concepts, relations, and propositions.

RETRIEVAL FROM SEMANTIC MEMORY

One study offers some evidence for the link between stored (remembered) information and cognitive structure (Rubenstein, Garfield, & Millikan, 1970). Subjects were presented with a mix of English words and nonsense words that varied in meaning, frequency of occurrence, and equivalence to English words. When a word was presented, the subject was to press a key for "yes" if he recognized it as an English word or another key for "no" if he did not recognize it. The time it took the subject to make a decision was recorded. The findings are just what one would expect if one views the subject as consulting his lexicon in his cognitive structure when retrieving information. High-frequency words were recognized more rapidly than low-frequency words; homographs (words such as *yard* and *still*, which have more than one meaning) were recognized more quickly than non-homographs because they have more storage places in the cognitive structure; and English words (which are high-frequency words compared to nonsense words) were recognized more quickly than nonsense words because their place in the cognitive structure is more readily identified. (The discussion on meaning and meaningfulness in Chapter Six offers related conclusions.)

Retrieval from semantic memory is also interesting because it suggests that the mind generates new information—that the mind is productive. Information retrieved from semantic memory often reappears in new combinations, not as originally experienced; such information may be retrieved as an inference, a rule that is generalized to new situations, a solution to a problem, or a newly formed concept. The experimenter who measures semantic memory is not concerned with word-for-word accuracy of recall; instead, he is concerned with the way recall is influenced by the overall theme or conceptual characteristics of the material. Accordingly, all responses are "correct," and good semantic recall depends on how well the meaning is identified by the learner.

This classification of the two kinds of memory (summarized from Tulving, 1972) provides a convincing case for the role of the mind in processing information and makes an important contribution to understanding the nature of thought. As Bartlett (1932) suggested many years ago, the mind can turn around on itself to generate new knowledge, to "know" something that was not learned directly.

TACIT AND EXPLICIT KNOWLEDGE

The rest of Chapter Seven shows that we know and use much more information than we can tell or than is apparent to even the most sophisticated observer (Polanyi, 1966). Such knowledge, which we have available and can use but of which we are more or less unaware, is called *tacit knowledge*. As Collins and Quillian (1972) have noted:

> There is ample evidence that a . . . tacit use of sizable amounts of stored information underlies all our visual perception, motor activity, problem solving, and so on (Bruner & Minturn, 1955; Polanyi, 1966). . . . [I]t has seemed best . . . to define the *full meaning*, for any particular person, of anything he reads, sees, thinks, or does, as all the information (stored in his head) that is in any way activated or processed when he deals with that thing (Quillian, 1968). If we define meaning in this way, then the full meaning of even simple stimuli or actions becomes very large indeed, and very large amounts of this meaning are always being tacitly processed as the person proceeds through the world . . ." [Collins & Quillian, 1972, p. 328].*

The knowledge that the individual has accessible to him at a given time is his *explicit knowledge*. It is what he can tell you about the world and about what he is conscious of. Explicit knowledge is often fragmentary, therefore less than one's tacit knowledge; it clearly lacks the richness of tacit knowledge, as we can see by trying to describe or analyze anything we know or do well.

> Repeat a word several times attending to the motion of your tongue and lips and to the sound you make, and soon the word will sound hollow and eventually lose its meaning. By concentrating on his fingers, a pianist can temporarily paralyze his movement. We can make ourselves lose sight of a pattern or physiognomy by examining its several parts under sufficient magnitude [Polanyi, 1966, p. 18].

These illustrations show that we can be aware of some features of experience but unaware of other features. Tacit knowledge probably occurs at all levels of consciousness. As the learner tries to shift from one to the other—that is, from the whole event to its description—he finds, as Polanyi has indicated, that he loses the general sense or meaning of the event.

ORGANIZATION AND RETRIEVAL

Could you learn a list of 100 words on a single presentation? Most people would consider it impossible, since it often takes learners 12 or more trials to learn a list of only eight or nine pairs of words that are low in

* From Collins, A. M., & Quillian, M. R. How to make a language user. In E. Tulving & W. Donaldson (Eds.), *Organization of Memory*. Copyright © 1972 by Academic Press, Inc. Reprinted by permission.

meaningfulness. However, if information is organized into conceptual categories, there is a marked increase in what can be recalled.

SUBJECTIVE ORGANIZATION

In an early experiment, Bousfield (1953) required his subjects to learn and recall a list of several words in four or five categories such as furniture (chair, table, lamp) or musical instruments (piano, accordion, violin). After the list was presented and removed, the subjects wrote down all the words they could remember in any order they chose. (This procedure is called *free recall*.) Bousfield found that subjects tended to recall the materials in an organized fashion around the major categories of the list. They had organized the list even though the words had been presented in random order.

In an interesting variation of this procedure, Seibel (1965, 1966) required learners to categorize 100 words in any way they wished on a study sheet. They were then briefly allowed to study the words as categorized; that is, the subjects studied the material in the way they, themselves, had organized it. Under these circumstances, the subjects were able to recall most of the words in the list after a single study trial. In pilot studies for my own experiments, I have shown subjects a random list of 50 words and 50 pictures. After a single presentation, the subjects were asked to recall the items by free recall. Without any instructions to do so, many subjects set up their own categories on the recall sheet and began to recall specific words or labels for pictures by filling in the categories just as Bousfield's subjects had done.

In a very early experiment described by Miller and Cofer (1972), Campos and Radecki (1928) used procedures similar to Bousfield's with one exception. During the free recall, subjects were given ample time to recall as many words as possible (non-cued recall). When they could recall no more words, the response sheet was taken away and the experimenter told the subjects the names of the categories and asked them to list all words belonging to that category without confining themselves to the original list of words (cued recall). There were 20 such categories; the subject was given one category at a time and was given one minute to write down as many words as possible from that category. This procedure resulted in additional items from the original list being recalled.

This study has been recently replicated by Tulving and Pearlstone (1966) in a more sophisticated experiment. The results were essentially the same as those found by Campos and Radecki: cued recall was greater than non-cued recall. Such studies imply that words not remembered in non-cued recall situations are available in memory but are inaccessible for retrieval. The studies also suggest that there are two retrieval processes, one concerned with the accessibility of higher-order units (that is, superordinate categories) and the other concerned with the accessibility of specific items in these larger categories (Tulving & Pearlstone, 1966).

These observations provide convincing evidence that learners do organize the material they have learned and that organization facilitates recall. Instructors can facilitate this process by presenting organized material, but without such organization, learners will organize information for themselves in ways that best suit their purposes. Even when information is organized (as in a textbook or lecture), good students will reorganize it rather than adopt an organization that seems arbitrary to them. Facts are not thrown into the memory as a potpourri of items without arrangement; they are structured. Once the learner can identify where in the cognitive structure he has placed the material, it becomes retrievable.

TOT RETRIEVAL

Given appropriate cues, stored information can be retrieved when needed. The observation that words flow spontaneously in oration, debate, and writing provides at least anecdotal support of the ready availability of ideas. But sometimes information cannot be retrieved; this may be due to a failure of retrieval rather than to so-called memory loss or decay. The tip-of-the-tongue (TOT) phenomenon illustrates this kind of retrieval failure (Brown & McNeill, 1966). Characteristically, one is certain that he knows a name or word; although he is agonizingly close to remembering it, he cannot quite remember it. The initial frustration is followed, upon recall, by a feeling of relief that is disproportionate to the often trivial nature of the word.

There are several important characteristics of this phenomenon. The person is aware that he does have the information. He knows many general characteristics of the word that he seeks. He attempts to find the new word by some search strategy. He feels helpless that he can't recall it. He is almost always certain that he will recall the word (and he usually does).

The TOT phenomenon seems to occur haphazardly. We may forget where we placed a book, so we search our memories by asking ourselves who might have borrowed the book, which other books we used with it, where we used it last. Or, if we have forgotten the unusual name of a shop, we search for sounds that correspond to the shop's name—*stool, flagpole, fat, fatstool* —and finally arrive at *Fatool's Specialty Shoppe*, the name of the store. In order to complete a crossword puzzle, we search for the name of a kind of humour based on a play on words. We know the word, but while it is on the tip of our tongue, we cannot retrieve it. Accordingly, we associate words with similar meanings and think of *limerick, comic, jokes, rhymes*, and *fun*. None of these is correct—we are certain of their incorrectness—but we puzzle over the word *fun*; it has a certain ring to it. We now change strategy, substituting new first letters for *fun* systematically in alphabetical order—*bun, dun, gun, hun, jun*—until we arrive at the target word, *pun.*

Since the TOT phenomenon is experienced in a variety of settings and since it occurs spontaneously and unpredictably, it is not easy to test experimentally. Accordingly, data on the particular retrieval processes involved are scarce. Nevertheless, Brown and McNeill (1966) have captured enough of the TOT phenomenon in a laboratory investigation to provide some flavor of the techniques people use in retrieving information.

Brown and McNeill presented their subjects with dictionary definitions of such low-frequency words as *ambergris, apse,* and *cloaca.* The subject's task was to identify the target word. Two examples illustrate the kinds of definitions used and may permit readers to experience this phenomenon:

> Favoritism shown to relatives or the bestowal of benefits because of familial relationship.

> An instrument used in navigation, especially at sea, for measuring angular distances.

Among such definitions were several words that each subject felt he knew (and did know). When he exhibited the TOT phenomenon in identifying a given word, he was asked to give his best guess as to the number of syllables in the word, the number of letters, and words with a similar sound and similar meaning to the word he had in mind. This study's results showed that learners were able to guess with considerable accuracy many of these features without identifying the word itself. They could guess the number of syllables in one-, two-, or three-syllable words, though longer words gave more difficulty. Letters in the first and last positions were guessed more accurately than those in the middle positions. There was some evidence that subjects put the stress on the correct first or second syllable. They could identify the suffix of the word with better-than-chance accuracy. They used two main strategies to arrive at the word: either they searched for words that sounded similar (that is, for the target word *sampan,* they produced *saipan, Cheyenne, sympoon,* and so on) or they combined two or three letters as *ex* in *extort* or *con* in *convene,* probably because with any specific letter, some combinations are more probable than others. As the subject approached the target word, he sifted out words that did not correspond to the target word even though he had not yet identified the target word itself.

As random as the TOT phenomenon seems in everyday experience, Brown and McNeill's study shows that people do not retrieve information randomly. Features of external cues are matched with features of the stored item without knowing exactly what that item is. This suggests that some information may be stored according to fragments of features rather than as whole words or ideas. The critical features of the input information are then identified as corresponding to or matched with the critical features of the stored item.

If these conclusions are correct, they may suggest why speech perception, reading, and sentence understanding take place so rapidly. We can obtain information about whole sentences or even paragraphs by attending to the critical features rather than to each sequential detail. Fluent readers read as though this were the case; they do not read each word. Speech typically is heard at 150 to 200 words per minute, but a subject can identify the meaning of speech that is spoken at 300 or more words per minute. Presumably, the subject identifies critical features of sounds. In both speech perception and reading, phrases or sentences are probably the units that provide cues to the base meaning.

Perhaps humans store information according to a complex set of critical features of words, meanings, and images rather than in terms of words or word combinations. However information is stored, it is clear that practice with retrieval processes (such as asking oneself questions) helps one to learn, at least intuitively, which processes are personally most efficient at retrieving information. (By the way, if you experienced the TOT phenomenon for the two definitions given earlier, the first and last letters of the target words are ne_ _ _ _sm and se_ _ _nt, respectively.)

SOME GENERAL RETRIEVAL PLANS

Learners use various strategies for encoding material as it is being learned. These strategies include generative rules, pegword systems, and hierarchical retrieval plans (Bower, 1972, pp. 111–117).* They have in common the use of cues for categories of information in the cognitive structure. All these strategies structure learning materials.

North, south, east, and _____?   Generative rules provide access to well-established categories with definite structural or grouping features. Once the rule is known, the learner can easily generate all possible cases of the category. For example, if you were asked to name the four suits in playing cards, you would answer "clubs, diamonds, hearts, and spades"; when asked to list kinds of silverware, you would say "fork, knife, tablespoon, teaspoon, sugarspoon, or ladle." Other such categories include the

---

* Adapted from Bower, G. A selective review of organizational factors in memory. In E. Tulving & W. Donaldson (Eds.), *Organization of Memory.* Copyright © 1972 by Academic Press, Inc. Used by permission.

names of planets, regions of the United States, or books of the Bible. Using generative plans another way, the learner might be presented with the numbers 1, 2, 4, 8, 16, 32. Once he has identified the underlying rule of "twice the previous number," he can easily generate not only the items learned initially but the remaining numbers as well, even though he had never seen or learned them before. Generative rules do not require the learner to remember all instances of learned material but only to check whether an instance fits the rule.

The method of loci and pegword systems in retrieval.   According to Bower (1970), one of the first records of mnemonic (memory) aids was by Cicero (in *De Oratore*). He told of a memory feat performed by the Greek poet, Simonides. Simonides had been commissioned to recite a poem at a banquet attended by many guests. Upon completing his oration, Simonides was called outside the banquet hall. During his brief absence, the building's roof collapsed, killing all of those at the banquet. So disastrous was the event that none of the corpses could be identified even by relatives. But Simonides was able to do so: from his vantage point during the oration, he had noted the location of each celebrant. By mentally revisiting each location, he named each corpse, thereby using what is now known as the method of loci for remembering—that is, maintaining a fixed arrangement of widely different features (such as the different rooms of a house) as an anchoring device for things to be remembered. Each object, person, or event is separately placed in each location. When events are to be recalled, one needs only to imagine walking through each location to identify the objects stored. One may speculate that the commonly used "in the first place . . . ," "in the second place . . . ," and so on had their origins in the method of loci.

Pegword systems function as artificial memory aids. An arbitrary known sequence of items is first established as a reference list against which new items are related or matched. Such lists may have been acquired already, as would be the mental image of one's home (the driveway, doorstep, foyer, living room, dining room, kitchen, bathroom, and bedroom) or the layout of a campus. Or, the reference list might be a jingle such as "one is a bun, two is a shoe, three is a tree, four is a door. . . ." The new list is learned by associating, or forming a link between, each new item and a corresponding item in the reference list. For example, in storing a grocery list, the learner may link "driveway—bread; doorstep—cereal; foyer—oranges; living room—lamb roast." Or he might say "one is a bun—bun and bread go together; two is a shoe—shoe is like a bowl, it can hold cereal; three is a tree—oranges grow on trees; four is a door—the lamb (roast) came in the door." When the learner wants to retrieve the shopping list, he either walks through his mental route if he is using the method of loci or he links his arbitrary reference list to what he intended to remember if he is using pegword systems.

Unpacking the hierarchy. Bower says a hierarchical plan has a function similar to the pegword plan, but the hierarchical plan is potentially much more powerful for practical learning situations. The learner or teacher using the hierarchical plan builds a strongly organized scheme of relationships in which sub-categories are nested in superordinate categories. (Such a scheme for minerals was presented in Figure 5-1.) Hierarchical plans are powerful because they consist of intrinsic meanings of the material being acquired and because they are meaningful to the learner. When organizing ideas, the learner may take larger categories and break them down into successively smaller units in order to organize information into clearly understood conceptual components.

Retrieval via a hierarchical plan might be analogous to the following description. Using Bower's mineral hierarchy (Bower, Clark, Lesgold, & Winzenz, 1969), the subject would first have to find a carton labeled "minerals" from among many different cartons in a large storage room. On opening the carton, the subject finds two covers for separate compartments: one is labeled "metals," and the other is labeled "stones." When these covers are removed, they each reveal two further sub-compartments: under "stones," there is a compartment for precious stones and one for common stones. Similarly under "metals," there is a compartment for precious metals and one for common metals. Having arrived at this point, the identification of specific items is disclosed: among the precious stones are rubies, diamonds, sapphires; the common stones include granite, limestone, and flagstone; the precious metals are gold, silver, and platinum; and the common metals include aluminum, iron, and copper.

OBLITERATIVE SUBSUMPTION

Whether he uses the method of loci, pegword systems, or a hierarchical plan, the learner uses categories that provide optimal entry into the cognitive structure via cues that make a wide range of associated ideas available. These ideas are scanned for items that meet the demands of the learner's intended purpose (for example, recalling items in serial order, recalling all ideas in a category, or recalling ideas necessary to answer a specific question). Whether the ideas are accessible at the time of recall depends on such variables as how well the structures were developed and the extensiveness of the categories.

When new learning is insufficiently anchored in an existing structure of knowledge, its details are soon forgotten. Ausubel (1968) has theorized that the details become obliterated by the more general concepts or subsumers. Robinson (1970) has suggested an exercise that will help you verify this point: it requires you to write down all you know about bronze. If you are not a chemistry major, you may be able to recall little more than that bronze is a metal, perhaps that it is an alloy, and, only because of its color, that it contains copper. You probably will be unable to name tin as the other metal in its composition.

It is also likely that, if you said it was an alloy, you forgot the distinctions among mixtures, solutions, and compounds and that alloys are solutions. Thus you would have forgotten that bronze is a solution of equally dispersed molecules of tin and copper. In other words, even though you might have learned what an alloy (the anchor or subsumer) is, the details have been obliterated by the generalities. Obliteration can be avoided by using a meaningfully learned structure like the one in Figure 7-1. It has the advantage of showing relationships so that particular features need not be memorized in rote fashion. Such structures are analogous to hierarchical plans.

FINDING THE THEMES IN RETRIEVAL

Connected discourse—a lecture, a speech, or a piece of reading material—has organizational properties just by virtue of being conveyed by language (Lachman & Dooling, 1968). In addition, a major characteristic of connected discourse is that it is guided by an overall plan or theme. This theme provides the basis for anticipating material still to be presented and for retaining material already presented. Later retrieval of the material depends on the quality of the plan or theme. Another characteristic of connected discourse is the presence of more or less well-formed sentences linked together in more or less connected sequences. These characteristics provide organizational properties to the material—through the syntactical arrangements of words in sentences, through the relationships emphasized among sentences, and through the meaning provided by different word orders and reconstruction of sentences.

In an experiment designed to investigate the effect of thematic organization on retrieval (Pompi & Lachman, 1967), 75 different words were presented in a meaningful order to one group and in a random order to another group. During the learning trial, each word was successively presented at a rate of one every two seconds. On a recall trial, the subjects were presented all of the 75 words plus a list of 150 distractor words, which included 75 words that could logically fit into the context of the original words and 75 other words that were related among themselves but to another theme.

Learners correctly identified more words from the test list when the words were presented during the learning trial in a meaningful order than when they were presented in a random order. The subjects were able to use

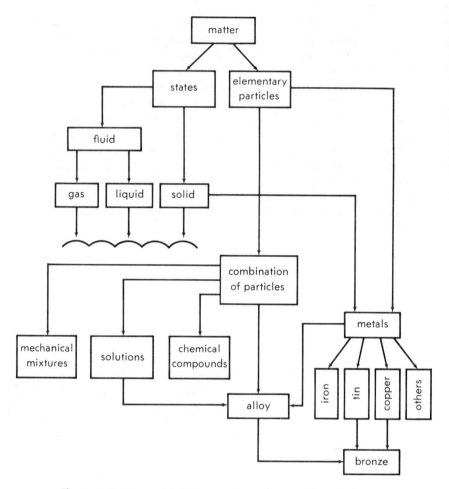

Figure 7-1. Map of initial cognitive structure in which the concept bronze was embedded. (From *Study Guide for Ausubel/Robinson School Learning: An Introduction to Educational Psychology*, prepared by Floyd G. Robinson. Copyright © 1970 by Holt, Rinehart and Winston, Inc. Reprinted by permission of Holt, Rinehart and Winston, Inc.)

the thematic organization for storing the material and retrieving it later according to the general cues provided by the theme. In addition, the learners identified more words incorrectly as being the original words when the incorrect words were presented in a way that fitted conceptually with the theme of the passage. This would happen only if subjects had used some skeletal outline representing a theme for learning the passage. Apparently they did, which demonstrates the importance not only of organizational factors in learning but also of language as an organizer of learning materials.

INTEGRATING AND CONSTRUCTING
SEMANTIC MEANINGS FROM SENTENCES

Recent ingenious studies by researchers Bransford and Franks (Franks & Bransford, 1971; Bransford, Barclay, & Franks, 1972; Bransford & Franks, 1970, 1971) have clarified the way sentences are combined and integrated to form complete ideas.

Only in the laboratory do people store and retrieve the exact material that served as a stimulus. For example, specific words, word-pairs, or sentences are presented to the subject, who is expected to copy and repeat them in exactly the same form they were presented—in a one-to-one correspondence between input and output. In real situations, especially in connected discourse, the learner uses information from several sentences to arrive at a meaning. Rarely does the learner recall the exact order of specific words.

The rock crushed the hut.   As an example, examine the following sentences (Bransford & Franks, 1971; Franks & Bransford, 1972). First, four ideas (level 4) are represented in a complex sentence:

> The rock that rolled down the mountain crushed the tiny hut at the edge of the woods.

These four ideas can also be represented by four simple sentences that each contain only one idea (level 1):

> The rock rolled down the mountain.
> The rock crushed the hut.
> The hut was tiny.
> The hut was at the edge of the woods.

Or, the ideas can be expressed by sentences that each contain two of the meanings (level 2):

> The rock that rolled down the mountain crushed the hut.
> The tiny hut was at the edge of the woods.

Or, the ideas can be expressed by sentences that combine three of the ideas (level 3):

> The rock that rolled down the mountain crushed the tiny hut.
> The rock that rolled down the mountain crushed the hut at the edge of the woods.

In an experiment, sets of four different ideas were prepared. Then only half of all possible items from each of levels 1, 2, and 3 were read to the learner. He was never presented level 4 sentences during this phase of the experiment. Next, the learner was given a recognition task. He was read the remaining sentences from levels 1, 2, and 3 as well as all level 4 items, which were all new sentences that the learner had not heard before. The sentences were presented in random order. As each sentence was read, the learner was to rate his confidence in having heard the sentence before on a scale ranging from +5 (complete confidence that the sentence had been heard before) to −5 (complete confidence that the sentence had not been heard before).

The result was that learners had most confidence in having heard the level 4 sentences—sentences that had not been presented! Confidence in having heard the item decreased regularly as the level of complexity of the sentence decreased—even to the point of confidence in not having heard level 1 items that had actually been presented.

Clearly, the learner does not retrieve sentences exactly as he heard them. He processes separate ideas into units and recognizes those sentences that contain all of the ideas. That the sentence is more complex than any presented to him doesn't seem to matter. The complex sentence permits an easily coded, cohesive expression of all information and is the best representation of what the person has learned; therefore, it is the most efficient sentence for storage.

Cognitive structures and retrieval.   In another study, Bransford, Barclay, and Franks (1972) demonstrated the influence of cognitive structure—what the learner already knows—in storing and retrieving information. They showed that the interpretation of sentences depends as much on the learner's knowledge as on the linguistic input represented by what is heard. Learners construct and generate meanings rather than merely interpret base structure meanings. Learners first heard descriptions (10 in all) such as the following one:

> There is a tree with a box beside it, and a chair is on top of the box. The box is to the right of the tree. The tree is green and extremely tall.

Then the learner was asked to recall which of the following sentences he had heard before:

> 1a. The box is to the right of the tree.
> 2a. The chair is to the right of the tree.
> 3a. The box is to the left of the tree.
> 4a. The chair is to the left of the tree.

or

> 1b. The tree is to the left of the box.
> 2b. The tree is to the left of the chair.

3b. The tree is to the right of the box.
4b. The tree is to the right of the chair.

Learners tended to pick (1a) 42 percent of the time, which was more often than they picked the others. However, 71 percent picked both (1a) and (1b). Both of these sentences agree with the original meaning, although only one of them had been heard before. The learners were equally divided in their selections of (1b) and (2b). Again, a total of 71 percent selected these two sentences as having been heard, yet neither one had been presented in the original sentences. In fact, the relationships in (1b) and (2b) are described from a different point of view than in the original sentences.

Learners apparently put more into the original sentence than was there to begin with. They derived a meaning for the entire set of sentences based on spatial placement of the tree, box, and chair; in other words, they assimilated the new information into their cognitive structures. From the basic relationships, they constructed other relationships that were not mentioned in the original sentences, which shows that linguistic representation is subordinated to semantic meaning.

SUMMARY

Research on memory shows that words and sentences form cues that allow the learner to tap his knowledge. Without knowledge, such words and sentences do not function as cues but with knowledge, language can be an aid to generating new information. However, what the reader/listener understands may not be the meaning intended or implied by the author/speaker. Adequate communication requires similar knowledge to be shared by both sender and receiver (Bransford, Barclay, & Franks, 1972).

PART
FOUR
PROCESSING
CONNECTED DISCOURSE

CHAPTER
EIGHT
LEARNING
TO READ

Reading is obviously a major educational concern. Much time is devoted to it in the elementary curriculum. Parents are concerned with the rate at which their children learn to read. Reading clinics are established at many universities to help poor readers at every educational level. Personality problems are often attributed to frustration encountered while learning to read and vice versa. Slow progress in reading is often blamed on conflicts between parent and child or between child and peers.

A DIFFERENCE OF OPINION

Methods for teaching children to learn to read vary widely, reflecting uncertainty about which method is best and simultaneously reflecting uncertainty about what reading really is. In one era, the whole-word method was popular; in another, it was the phonics method. The initial-teaching alphabet was used at one time, word recognition at another. Silent reading is advocated on one hand, while oral reading is encouraged on the other. The language-experience procedure was used at the turn of the century, abandoned a decade later, then picked up again in the 1960s as a new approach. Sometimes a carefully worked out system that integrates all approaches is used. Different aspects of learning to read may be structured to occur at different times; sometimes experience may precede phonics; sometimes phonics may precede experience. Some authorities advocate permissiveness when the child is achieving reading skill; others insist carefully structured situations are best because they enable children of 3 or 4 to read. Such contrasts are endless.

Chapter Eight presents an approach to reading that is compatible with the cognitive-structure approach to linguistics that this book has taken.

Letter recognition, word recognition, phonics, and control of eye movements are important for reading, but the most important component of reading readiness has yet to be identified. Certainly a child cannot learn to read without recognizing a word, decoding its meaning, or moving his eyes from left to right over the printed line. At some point in the development of reading, close approximations to accurate spelling may be important, but this skill is more important for writing than for reading. Learning to break the code of phoneme-grapheme correspondences through phonics is probably helpful at some stage in reading, but its value as a formal educational procedure for the beginning reader remains to be validated. The initial teaching alphabet, in which traditional word forms are replaced by symbol codes based on letters and sounds, may be used as a crutch for early learning but must be replaced eventually by the traditional alphabet.

A DEFINITION OF READING

The apparent chaos in recommendations for teaching reading may be due to too many different activities being grouped under the label *reading*. If so, a definition of reading will clarify on which activities we must focus. Reading is gaining meaning from the sentence and is a synthesis of many component skills rather than a mere summation of all the skills and knowledge a pupil has; that is, these skills form a system. Reading is not word recognition, spelling, or phonic analysis, which may indicate reading readinesses but are not reading. Nor is reading serial processing—merely sounding out or recognizing letters or words one by one. This is not even a necessary process; fluent readers do not use it. Reading is not saying the sound that corresponds to each of the words in a sentence. Reading may involve vocalization in the early stages but it is not necessary for reading.

HOW DOES A GOOD READER READ?

What does it mean to say that reading is comprehension? There are three fundamental components: the input—that is, the symbols on the page; the cognitive structure—that is, the readers' immediate and long-term experiences; and a strategy for linking the two—that is, the transformational processes for arriving at the base structure of what is being read.

Although serial processing is not characteristic of fluent readers, many teaching methods—especially those involving oral reading—teach children to read word by word. Good readers use some method of scanning lines, picking up meaningful cues from words, phrases, and sentences. They do not read each word but can pick out the important, meaningful words. Certainly good readers do not read every letter, as we see when we catch our own typographical errors only on a third reading. Reading, then, involves rapid scanning and guesses as to the meaning. As the reader proceeds, words contribute to the meaning of phrases and the phrases contribute to the meaning of sentences. If this process does not make sense, the reader may then make *regressive* fixations—he may look back at other words that enable him to restructure the sentence's meaning—which again indicates that the reader processes the meaning of the sentence as a unit rather than one word at a time.

Fast reading is essential because short-term memory (STM) holds material only a short time without continuous rehearsal. The ploddingly slow reader strains his STM. By the time he reaches the end of a sentence, he has forgotten its beginning, which he needs for understanding. Yet those basal readers and teaching methods based on letter and word recognition stress precise mechanics of reading rather than comprehension. Young learners are taught to read each word and are corrected for oral mistakes without regard to the kind of error made. After considerable reinforcement from teachers, habits associated with such techniques are very difficult to break.

Besides reading rapidly, readers must also differentiate features of a word or words rather than recognize individual letters. Furthermore, readers must be aware of cues from the syntactical arrangement of the surface structure of the sentence. Some feeling for grammatical classes of words and phrase structure helps even the very young reader, but an incorrect word may be reasonable in terms of the sentence's base structure. Requiring beginning readers to correct such errors may be frustrating and futile.

WHAT DO READING ERRORS MEAN?

Goodman (1970) demonstrates the importance of reading for meaning. His figures allow us to compare the interpretation of errors from a common-sense approach (which holds that readers must read each word precisely) with a psycholinguistic approach (which considers what the reader is trying to do). Figure 8–1 shows the errors made by a fourth-grade child reading from a sixth-grade book. The book is a little advanced for him and thus tests the limits of his reading ability. By examining the child's errors, Goodman infers reasons for the errors. For example, the first error can be considered a substitution since both words are noun markers. The error was not made because the pupil didn't recognize *your*, since he said it correctly in the preceding phrase. The substituted word made sense to the reader and in fact doesn't change the meaning of the sentence. A fluent reader would not correct his error in this case, so why should the beginning reader be forced to do so if the purpose of reading is for comprehension?

Next, *hoped* was substituted for *opened*; this error may be based on graphemic similarities and may reflect the child's French-Canadian background. We can consider it an intelligent error, since both words are verbs. Since the sentence didn't make sense, the reader corrected (©) his initial guess. Substituting *what it means* for *word meanings first* is an excellent example of transformational processes. It attests to the value of Goodman's acute analysis of errors. Other errors such as the child's attempts to pronounce *philosophical* suggest the reader's knowledge of phonic rules.

"If it bothers you to think of it as baby sitting," my father said, "then

don't think of it as baby sitting. Think of it as homework. Part of your

education. You just happen to do your studying in the room where ~~your~~ the

baby brother is sleeping, that's all." He helped Mother with her coat, and

then they were gone.

So education it was! I ~~opened the~~ hoped © a dictionary and picked out a word that

sounded good. ⌠PH "Phil/oso/phi/cal!" ✛ yelled. Might as well study ~~word~~ what

it means   1. Phizo 2. Phiso/soophical   his

~~meanings first~~. "~~Philosophical~~: showing calmness and courage in ~~the~~ face of

1. fort 2. future 3. futshion

ill fortune." I mean I really yelled it. I guess a fellow has to work off steam

once in a while.

Figure 8-1. A passage that shows a fourth-grade pupil's errors in reading. (From Goodman, K. S. Reading: A psycholinguistic guessing game. In H. Singer & R. B. Ruddell [Eds.], *Theoretical Models and Processes of Reading.* Copyright © 1970 by the International Reading Association. Reprinted by permission K. S. Goodman and the International Reading Association.)

Figure 8–2 is another of Goodman's examples that illustrates how syntactical arrangements affect reading performance. The story is being read by a first-grade child. The story *Ride In* is from a second pre-primer; it attempts to increase word recognition with little consideration for syntactical arrangement. *Stop and Go* is a third pre-primer. It is more difficult than *Ride In*, but the sentences, because of their syntax, are more meaningful; the sentences relate a story.

The child made proportionately more errors in the first story than he did in the second story. The common-sense approach would be to drill the pupil on the words he missed. But in the second, more complex passage, the reader had no trouble with words of equal difficulty because of the passage's stronger syntax. Goodman notes that substituting *toy* for train is natural for this reader because *too* was used for toy (airplane). A train is *toy* and a plane is *too*. Although *too* effectively conveyed the meaning, note that it created a little difficulty when the child tried to read toy train in line 2.

Goodman's work shows that even very young children can profitably use syntax when learning to read. It also shows that reading, as contrasted with word recognition, is oriented toward gaining meaning. Furthermore, Goodman's work shows that errors are not sheer mechanical blunders; teachers should distinguish between reasonable errors and errors that lead to confusion and correct only the latter. Teachers should provide reading materials that are sensible stories rather than nonsense phrases and that are written in the child's language rather than in the artificial language that is typical of many primers.

Ride In	*Stop and Go*
Run	
~~Ride~~ in, Sue.	Jimmy said, "Come here, Sue,
Run	too
~~Ride~~ in here.	Look at my ~~toy~~ (train.)
Come here	
~~Here~~ I ~~come,~~ Jimmy.	See it go.
Can come	toy
~~And here I~~ (stop.)	Look at my little ~~train~~ go."
	toy
	Sue said, "Stop the ~~train~~.
	come
	Stop it ~~here~~, Jimmy."
	toy
	Jimmy said, "I can stop the ~~train~~.
	toy
	See the ~~train~~ stop."
	too
	Sue said, "Look at my ~~toy~~.
	toy
	It is in the ~~train~~.
	too
	See my little red ~~toy~~, Jimmy.

toy
It can ride in the ~~train~~."

toy
Jimmy said, "See the ~~train~~ go.

Look at it go."

Suzie   too
~~Sue~~ said, "Look at my little red ~~toy~~.

toy
See it go for a ~~train~~ ride."

Suzie   too
~~Sue~~ said, "My little red ~~toy~~!

said   too
Jimmy, ∧ my ⌐ ~~toy~~ is not here.

toy
It is not in the ~~train~~.

toy
Stop the ~~train~~, Jimmy.

too
Stop it and look for my ~~toy~~."

Figure 8-2. A passage that shows a first-grade pupil's errors in reading. The passages are from *Ride In* (Betts, 1963), a second pre-primer, and *Stop and Go* (Betts & Welch, 1963), a third pre-primer. (From Goodman, K. S. Reading: A psycholinguistic guessing game. In H. Singer & R. B. Ruddell [Eds.], *Theoretical Models and Processes of Reading.* Copyright © 1970 by the International Reading Association. Reprinted by permission of K. S. Goodman and the International Reading Association.)

THE READER'S CONTRIBUTION TO READING

Goodman's work shows that the reader contributes as much to reading through his cognitive structure as the written symbols do. The fluent reader substitutes words, paraphrases sentences, skips many words, is guided in fixations (that is, stopping his eye movements when reading) on word sequences that probably correspond to phrase markers, and often depends on fragments of letter or word features. Compared to the less fluent reader, the fluent reader is more efficient in his use of fixations, and he makes fewer regressive fixations. These processes are affected by what the reader knows about syntactical constructions (compare reading English with reading a foreign language) and about the world in general (compare reading familiar materials with reading highly technical materials).

Reading style varies. First, there are individual differences in reading rate. Some people adapt their rates to the difficulty of the material, while others read all materials at the same rate. Second, there are differences in the degree to which readers elaborate on reading material; some people freely add their own meanings to what they read, while others read for the literal sense of what the author intended. Third, there are individual differences in mechanical aspects of reading: in fixations; in scanning; in dependence on figural characteristics of letters, words, or sentences; and in selecting what material to focus on. These and other reading styles relate the reading material to the reader's cognitive structure. Reading style depends on what one thinks reading is. If one has been taught to read letters and words without error, he will use short fixations and read slowly. If one's goal in reading is to gain meaning, he will probably scan and use information-processing techniques.

A PROGRAM FOR INSTRUCTION ON READING

What program of reading instruction do these conclusions suggest? Although research data are lacking, a reading program should consider the following points:

1. Anyone trying to force (however gently) a retarded or slow reader to read better or faster will receive little reward for his efforts. The child who is forced to go through prescribed routines will become increasingly frustrated with reading rather than more accomplished, and his self-esteem and interest in reading may both decrease; records of reading clinics support this conclusion. Furthermore, when children are released from restrictive teaching practices, they often learn to read soon thereafter. Most children in school do learn to read at some level: some, despite all efforts, never make more than minimal progress, although the poor reader often reads material that interests him (comic books, for example) amazingly rapidly. Other children learn to read without instruction. Despite these findings, schools spend much time and energy on accelerating reading ability. Perhaps reading (defined as getting meaning) is not a necessary part of the curriculum in the early grades. Perhaps formal instruction in reading could be postponed or eliminated entirely. Are we taking away valuable time from other learning activities by prematurely making the child spend one to two hours each day in learning to read? Have we unrealistically made reading into the sacred cow of education?

2. A rich cognitive structure is absolutely necessary if one is to read for meaning. A wide variety of experiences is helpful. Since the young child

is an efficient assimilator of information around him, he asks questions, explores, and translates; he likes to listen to stories and to look at pictures. We can channel these interests during this period of the child's life to help the child build a rich cognitive structure. Many media besides reading can help the young reader acquire knowledge at his own pace. Television, video tape, demonstrations, or field trips can all provide information and hold the child's interest without requiring reading skills. These media can provide him with experience in relating spoken material to action. Furthermore, story-telling offers the child direct experience in extracting themes (though he need not be given direct instruction), in hearing and speaking the language and its transformations, and in developing images. These media can be used in any subject area; if reading were de-emphasized, more of teachers' and pupils' time could be devoted to other subject areas.

3. Word recognition, spelling, and phonics are recognized as important aspects of learning to read, but they are not necessarily important components of instructional practice for teaching reading. Word recognition can be formally taught by drill and similar techniques, but it can also be taught indirectly. Even the very young child likes to try to read road signs. He is elated when he receives a letter addressed to him and soon recognizes his written or printed name. If name tags are placed on chairs or if items are labeled in his room, he will happily comply with the teacher's request to associate the printed symbol with the article. The pupil is more likely to be motivated to engage in such reading games than in textbook reading drills. The possible variety of exercises like this is limited only by one's imagination. Alphabetizing can be taught using similar techniques, as can phonics. Phonics is most helpful to the person who is already a reader rather than to one who is beginning to read, and the child's readiness to grasp the relationships easily is an essential consideration here. These are two good reasons for postponing the teaching of phonics until after the child has begun to read. The second year of school might be an appropriate average time, although opinions on this vary. We may know more about teaching phonics than about teaching any other facet of reading, so teachers are likely to reach their objectives efficiently. However, phonics should not be confused with reading but should be considered an aid for the more advanced reader. Phonics is useful in all language arts—spelling, writing, and speaking. Its function is not restricted to reading, and its teaching should not interfere with the teaching of initial skills required for fluent reading.

Phonics might be combined with spelling, another important school subject. By combining the two, the teacher can make the best use of the linguists' contribution to understanding of word construction. In addition, the characteristics of letters and words can be singled out when necessary for quick recognition and identification. When words have single or multiple definitions, they can be indicated. However, if phonics is included in reading, the learner's task is complicated.

4. Writing, speaking, and listening are all related to reading since they use words, combine words into grammatically correct sentences that express ideas, and combine sentences into paragraphs that contain related ideas—all of which translate experiences into spoken and written form. Writing shows how words in books are used. Much about reading can be learned through speaking and listening without the pressures and poor habits that tend to accompany the forced teaching of reading. A procedure suggested earlier by Huey (1908), is currently being revived as a technique called *language experience*. Pupils write short stories of their experiences and either read them aloud to other pupils or combine the stories into reading books, or both. Pressure to read is de-emphasized, but the stories are available for pupils to read whenever they want. For example, pupils may read the stories to themselves or they might ask other pupils to read to them; even in kindergarten, some children can read to others. This procedure has the advantage of providing meaningful reading material that is written in the child's own language style. When the stories are read by other children, non-readers are motivated to learn to read by seeing a model.

5. Syntax should be considered even in the first primers. Most basal readers contain stilted sentences that no child would use. Huey (1908) suggested that slight indentations on alternate lines would help the young reader, but this reasonable recommendation has not been used, although many primers contain completely irregular arrangements of type. Similarly, the young reader's attention is captivated by line drawings like those found in comic books, for example (Huey, 1908). Yet primers often contain complex pictures that may appeal only to adults. Complicated pictures do not seem to correspond to a child's experience. Large type may also help the beginning reader, who may not be able to make the short movement—that is, the sweeps of the eyes between fixations—required in reading.

6. Most important, illustrations in readers should relate to the story being told by arousing interest in the story or clarifying it.

7. Above all, to encourage rapid, enthusiastic reading, reading material must have intrinsic interest and underlying continuity reflected in a general theme and related subthemes.

SUMMARY

The pressures that counteract rapid reading do not have to be built in to reading instruction during the early school years. Pupils can be allowed to grow into fluent, comprehending readers at their own pace. In summary, I suggest that: (1) The early school years (kindergarten through second or third grade) should be devoted to structured, rich, varied experiences that contribute to the growth of the cognitive structure. (2) Early language instruction should consist primarily of experiences in listening, speaking, and writing. (3) Word recognition should be incorporated into the child's education in informal ways. (4) The child should be exposed to reading materials but should not be forced to read them, although he might be encouraged to do so by allowing other pupils of his age to read aloud, thereby serving as models. (5) A poor grade or evaluation on reading skills might frustrate or lower the self-esteem of a child. Teachers should focus on the child's strengths. (6) Formal instruction in phonics should be postponed until the child has some elementary skill in writing, spelling, and reading and thus can see what phonics is all about. (7) Formal instruction in reading should be directed toward habits that permit rapid, fluent reading—scanning, using key features for fixations, and identifying the meaning of sentences and paragraphs. This means that formal reading instruction, if needed at all, should be postponed until much later than the first grade, when it is usually introduced today. The school should stimulate rather than try to accelerate the acquisition of reading skills.

CHAPTER NINE
LEARNING FROM TEXTUAL MATERIALS

After speech, reading is the learner's most important skill. Learning from textual materials obviously depends on the materials themselves, but it also depends on the organization of supplementary material, behavioral objectives, the teacher's instructions, and questions interjected in the text or presented by the teacher. All affect the direction learning will take. In the end, what the pupil learns depends on what he is presented (the course content), what he brings to the learning situation in the form of acquired knowledge (what he knows), the way his knowledge is organized (his cognitive structure), and the way he processes material. The teacher intentionally or unintentionally encourages the learner to use different processes. At the least meaningful level, the learner may be encouraged only to parrot material as it was presented; or, he may be asked to make simple associations between sequential ideas, relating only one idea to the next. At a conceptually meaningful level, the learner may be encouraged to abstract important ideas, to form concepts, or to form relationships among concepts. At the inferential level of meaning, the learner uses the information in new ways—that is, he derives new deductions, inferences, or creative solutions to problems, all of which represent higher levels of cognitive processing. At this level of thinking, he could apply his knowledge to problems he has never before encountered. At this level, comprehension is essential.

INFLUENCING COMPREHENSION

To comprehend requires both the information a learner receives and the information he already has. A learner does not simply interpret a sentence's surface structure. Such factors as the prosodic features of speech facilitate interpretation; words in a passage with a clear theme are recalled more easily than words not linked by a theme; but, more important, incorrectly recalled words are also somehow clearly related to the overall theme. The learner seems to depend on much more than the information provided in the specific words, syntax, or semantics of a given sentence.

VERBAL CONTEXT

In an early study by Cofer (1951), the four words

add, subtract, multiply, increase

were presented to learners with the instruction to identify the word that did not belong. This seemingly simple task has two answers. The series of words can refer to either arithmetical operations or increasing magnitude. Which classification one uses determines the word that does not belong. In the context of increasing magnitude, *subtract* would be excluded; in the context of arithmetical operations, *increase* would be excluded. The first of the two unambiguous words to appear in the series seems to determine the classification to be used. In this example, *subtract* is clearly an arithmetical operation and *increase* is clearly related to increasing magnitude; they are unambiguous. However, *add* and *multiply* are ambiguous, they can refer to either arithmetical operations or increasing magnitude. In the preceding series, *increase* is most likely to be excluded since *subtract*, the other unambiguous word, came first and determined the context. However, in the following series, *subtract* will be eliminated.

add, increase, multiply, subtract

Similarly, when a word like *theory* is rated for concreteness or abstractness, it is usually rated as relatively abstract when it stands alone as a single word; however, when it is placed in the context of a series of words related to experimentation (*theory, apparatus, experimentation, analysis, report*), it is rated as much more concrete. In short, the meaning of words is influenced by their context.

CONTEXT AND CONCEPT ACQUISITION

Direct experience in looking at, touching, or handling objects helps children in the early stages of development to acquire concepts. As children acquire further knowledge, particularly about language, their ability to acquire concepts increases. A new word's meaning can often be identified by its place in a sentence or a paragraph. The meanings of known words become tools for identifying and generating meanings of new words. The person does not have to depend on external experience alone.

A study by Werner and Kaplan (1950) demonstrated the use of context in acquiring concepts. Artificial words were grouped into sets of six sentences, and then children from 8½ to 13½ years old were asked to interpret the artificial word. For example:

A *corplum* may be used for support.
Corplums may be used to close off an open space.
A *corplum* may be long or short, thick or thin, strong or weak.

You must have enough space in your bookcase to *hudray* your library.
Jane had to *hudray* the cloth so the dress would fit Mary.
If you eat well and sleep well, you will *hudray*.

The correct meaning of the artificial word cannot be identified by sound (a perceptual feature); contextual cues from all three sentences must be used—for example, is the word a noun or a verb? (*Stick* and *increase*, or *grow*, are the correct substitutes for the artificial words in these examples.)

Young children make the mistake of using part of one of the sentences as a definition of the word; they say, "A *corplum* is something you use to make a fence," or "*Hudray* is something you do to cloth." As they proceed through the sentences in a set, each mistake of this kind extends the word's meaning in a general way so that a phrase that fits one sentence will fit the others. One child said, "If you sleep well, but not too much, you don't get overlazy; so you leave room for more sleep—so you leave space" (see the sentences in the *hudray* set).

The error of using part of the sentence as a definition decreases sharply with age and disappears by the time the child is 10½ years old. The error of extending meaning still appears frequently at 12½ years of age. The systematic nature of these errors suggests that the child is processing sentences; he alters them to make them comprehensible.

The fact that developmental changes do occur in the ability to link semantic and grammatical aspects of language reflects the child's growing comprehension of grammatical structure. The positions of words in sentences do distinguish one word from another—that is, whether it is a noun or a verb. Even very young children seem to be able to use aspects of the surface structure as clues to the role of each word in the sentence (Braine, 1963). Other clues come from grammatical transformations, which may account for the kinds of errors subjects made in the preceding study (Werner & Kaplan, 1950). While children can use grammatical rules at a very early age to construct their own sentences, the more difficult task of interpreting the meaning of sentences requires additional, more complex rules.

PROVIDING CONTEXTS

Studies conducted during the 1930s and 1940s showed that one's attitude toward a communication depended not only on its contents but also on its presumed author (Sherif, 1935; Lorge, 1936; Lewis, 1941). One study attributed a prose passage to two different authors, gave one group of subjects the passage by one author and another group the passage by another author. The authors—Thomas Jefferson and Lenin—differed in prestige. Other factors—such as the length of the passage, its credulity, and its affective objectivity—were controlled. Clearly, different contexts were provided for interpreting the same passage.

The general finding was that the prestige associated with the author's name increased or decreased the acceptability, favorableness, and general value of the passage's ideas (Lorge, 1936). Lewis (1941) qualified this conclusion by saying that prestige influences evaluation only for ambiguous material—material that has more than one meaning or can be as easily attributed to one author as to another. Subjects will not change their attitude about statements that clearly conflict with what they know to be true, but attitudes that can be viewed as readily from one frame of reference as from another can be readily repatterned.

Let's look at the influence of context in a recent study. Read the following passage only once. Immediately after reading it do two things: (1) rate its comprehensibility on a scale of 1 to 7 (1 = very incomprehensible, 4 = in between, and 7 = very comprehensible); (2) jot down as many of the ideas as you can recall without reviewing the paragraph again.

> The procedure is actually quite simple. First, you arrange things into different groups. Of course, one pile may be sufficient depending on how much there is to do. If you have to go somewhere else due to lack of facilities that is the next step, otherwise you are pretty well set. It is important not to overdo things. That is, it is better to do too few things at once than too many. In the short run this may not seem important but complications can easily arise. A mistake can be expensive as well. At first the whole procedure will seem complicated. Soon, however, it will become just another facet of life. It is difficult to foresee any end to the necessity for this task in the immediate future, but then one can never tell. After the procedure is completed one arranges the materials into different groups again. Then they can be put in their appropriate places. Eventually they will be used once more and the whole cycle will have to be repeated. However, that is part of life.*

If your ratings were similar to those of Bransford and Johnson's subjects, you probably rated the passage as somewhat incomprehensible and you could recall only two or three ideas.

If a context is established for the passage—if you discover that the passage is about washing clothes—you will find it to be very understandable upon rereading. Bransford and Johnson also found that when the context

* From Bransford, J. D., & Johnson, M. K. Conceptual prerequisites for understanding: Some investigations of comprehension and recall. *Journal of Verbal Learning and Verbal Behavior*, 1972, **11**, 717–726. Copyright © 1972 by Academic Press, Inc. Reprinted by permission.

was established before the passage was read, both ratings and recall were twice as favorable as when no context was established before reading.

Note that the passage's semantic properties by themselves did not communicate the meaning to you. An inappropriate context—such as working on an assembly line—would have hindered your comprehension and retrieval even more than a neutral context—such as arranging into groups—would have. With no context, you probably searched for an idea of what the passage was about.

The reader, of course, does get some meaning from syntactic and semantic markers, but when sentences are unclear, readers will make assumptions in order to clarify ideas. Consider this sentence (Bransford & Johnson, 1972):

> Bill is able to come to the party tonight because his car broke down.

If you are asked what this sentence means, you do not simply break it into two parts, leaving out *because*. Instead, you will probably construct an elaborate set of assumptions oriented around *because*—perhaps something like, "Bill was invited to a party but declined because he was leaving town. However, his car broke down; since he had no readily available transportation for a long trip and since the party was within walking distance, he was able to come to the party."

Obviously, readers interpret sentences according to the way the new material interacts with what they already know. The sentence's structure provides some cues—for example, the word *because* in the preceding example—but the reader must create a situation that brings all elements into a unified, meaningful pattern. Ausubel (1968) has proposed that the learner can be assisted by the use of *advance organizers* to integrate what he already knows with new learning.

ADVANCE ORGANIZERS

Learning materials can be organized by introducing them properly: one introduction might stress the objectives to be attained during reading; another might summarize the material's contents and present a hierarchical organization of it. Both approaches are called advance organizers.

Objectives.   Behavioral objectives describe what the material to be learned contains and by what criteria the student can evaluate his performance. If they are too specific, they may lead the student to overlook general ideas in favor of details—that is, they may encourage him to study simply to reproduce facts. Broad objectives encourage the student to organize materials into hierarchical structures and to derive implications or applications from them.

Summaries. Ausubel defines *advance organizers* as introductory summaries. To illustrate, in studies by Ausubel and Fitzgerald (1962), subjects read a passage on how Buddhism treats such topics as life, death, God, sin, and truth. One group was given a historical advance organizer that briefly reviewed the history of Buddhism. Another group was given a comparative advance organizer that compared Buddhism and Christianity. A third group was given an expository advance organizer that summarized the details and organization of the passage itself. The expository organizer was more helpful than the others, particularly for learners with low verbal and analytic ability. The expository organizer also helped those who had no previous background in the subject area, while the comparative organizer helped those who had some background in a related area.

Teaching methods. The relationship between what one knows and one's acquisition of new material is apparent in comparisons between learning through discovery and expository teaching methods with college students (Greeno, 1972). Discovery tends to be an effective procedure when the learner has a fund of information relevant to the solution of the problem. The expository procedure is effective when new material is introduced to learners who have had no previous knowledge or experience with the subject. Discovery seems to function in a similar way to comparative advance organizers: both help to incorporate new material into the existing cognitive structure. The expository teaching method is similar to the expository advance organizer: both help to establish a cognitive structure that will help the learner acquire the new material; they establish subsumers that function as focal points for organizing the new material.

ORGANIZATION IN LEARNING MATERIALS

Cognitive structures vary on at least two dimensions, each of which affects new learning (Greeno, 1972): *internal connectedness* refers to the clarity, strength, and complexity of the hierarchical organization of subsumers; *external connectedness* refers to the strength and clarity of the way the material is linked to other areas of knowledge. The meaningfulness of new material depends largely on external connectedness.

With increasing understanding, segments of cognitive structure are organized into larger and increasingly more inclusive categories that link one hierarchy with another. When these segments remain separated, compartmentalized, or unstructured, it means the learner has been unable to relate material from several frames of reference. Broadly inclusive, highly structured categories permit crossover of information, allowing flexibility; that is, the learner can make more combinations out of three well-defined concepts than from a single amorphous mass of data.

Inflexibility can often be overcome by showing the relationship between two parts of a structure. Thus the learner who sees that stones and metals are both part of the larger category of minerals can differentiate stones and metals but can also see that they share many features. Partitioning and differentiation increase the amount of information at his command. Similarly, while a learner may know two separate parts of the binomial theorem, he may not be able to combine them unless he realizes the conceptual relationship between them. Greeno (1972) has demonstrated that when learners see this relationship, they can solve problems involving the two parts of the formula; without this insight, learners were unsuccessful. Such integration of information is essential for problem-solving and creativity.

Any discipline is organized around key concepts that function as organizers for component ideas. Chapter titles of introductory psychology texts indicate their organization, usually under such traditional concepts as motivation, transfer, and retention. Each concept can be sub-divided further; for example, retention can be broken down into short-term memory, long-term memory, and retrieval systems. Persons who are well acquainted with the field use such categories for organizing new information, and the specialist uses still further subdivisions and differentiations. The more knowledge one has, the more he can subdivide information into stable categories. Fields such as physics that have the benefit of generations of experience have a relatively stable organization; newer fields, such as the social sciences, have less stable organizations, which become more stable as the field develops.

THE USE OF ADJUNCT QUESTIONS

Adjunct study questions interspersed throughout reading material help readers to process text materials, thereby encouraging what Rothkopf (1970) has called *mathemagenic behaviors*, or "activities that give birth to learning." Mathemagenic positive behaviors facilitate learning and retention; mathemagenic negative behaviors interfere with learning. The latter category includes daydreaming, attempts to reduce anxiety, attempts to overcome factors associated with fatigue, displays of temper, or short-cutting the learning process. Positive mathemagenic behaviors are encouraged by using behavioral objectives and advance organizers and organizing materials.

SEARCH BEHAVIORS

Some ingeniously contrived experiments have examined the effects of organization of content in the passage itself (Frase & Silbiger, 1970; Frase, 1969, 1968a, 1968b). The learning materials in these experiments consisted of passages that described the terrain, distance from the Earth, and atmospheric color of 10 planets. The passages were organized either in terms of the planet or in terms of the planet's attributes:

Organization by Name	*Organization by Attribute*
Ergama has two moons.	Ergama has two moons.
Ergama is three light years from Earth.	Urpropta has three moons.
Ergama has blue terrestrial features.	Ergama is three light years from Earth.
Urpropta has three moons.	Urpropta is one light year from Earth.
Urpropta is one light year from Earth.	Ergama has blue terrestrial features.
Urpropta has orange terrestrial features.	Urpropta has orange terrestrial features.

In one experimental condition, the learner was presented with several attributes arranged according to the concept name, as shown in the column titled "Organization by Name." In another experimental condition, the learner was shown the variation of each attribute for all planets, as in the column titled "Organization by Attribute."

The learner was instructed to find the concept name associated with a given attribute, such as "Which planet has orange features?" He was required to engage in search processes—that is, he was to find, from among many items, a single piece of information. Often, the learner was given a task that could not be completed from the information given—for example, the name or attribute might have been missing, as in the question, "Is there a planet two light years away from Earth?" The latter procedure assures that the learner will pay attention to more of the items and, together with the manipulation of organization, provides a sure way of influencing search processes.

Several interesting findings have emerged from these studies. (1) When material was organized by name, learners acquired more information about the attributes; when it was organized by attributes, they learned more about names. (2) Searching improved the acquisition of incidental information. If the learner was asked to find a planet with a given attribute, he would also learn the attributes of other planets. (3) When the material is presented to learners in a random format they tend to structure it in terms of concepts rather than attributes, as their free recall shows (Schultz & DiVesta, 1972). (4) As in the Ausubel and Fitzgerald (1962) study, subjects who received advance organizers retained increasingly more material over consecutive trials than a control group without advance organizers.

Connected discourse may be organized according to either a logical structure or a psychological structure. Logical structure would use hierarchical categories and sub-categories; careful outlines or charts might be used to clarify this organization. Psychological structure would focus more on the learner's readiness: first, motivation would be stimulated; second, the learner would be prepared to understand basic concepts; third, the learner would be provided with several opportunities to organize the material in his own way; finally, he would be asked to summarize the presentation in his own terms. Logical organization parallels the technical or professional organization of a discipline, while psychological organization parallels the learner's readiness to understand the presentation. Each structure affects what the learner will absorb because each structure encourages the learner to use different learning processes.

Specific and general questions.   Once advance organizers have been presented and the learner's attention has been obtained, the teacher must consider what other stimuli can direct the learner's activities. A frame in a programmed learning text is one such stimulus; it asks questions that determine what the learner will learn and remember and thereby helps him to focus his attention. The learner's answers are either reinforced or incorrect answers are identified, helping the learner find the correct answer and be reinforced. Learning activities generated by such programs are entirely under student control (Rothkopf, 1970).

Study questions, whether or not they are part of programmed learning, help the learner to make necessary discriminations while he is reading. Generally, a question that is too easy is less effective than a question that requires more search activity (Rothkopf & Coke, 1966).

The wording of questions is also important. For example, Frase (1968b) asked learners to underline all words in a passage that answer such specific questions as "When did Columbus discover America?" When a statement like "Columbus discovered America in 1492" appeared in the text, learners should have underlined all of it, but most of them underlined only "1492," the response. Some learners underlined only the stimulus, "Columbus discovered America." Typically, learning material must be used by relating the stimulus terms to the response terms. Thus, on examinations students are required to remember not only *1492* but also that it was *Columbus who discovered America in 1492.* If students pay primary attention only to the response term, the likelihood of optimal performance is decreased.

When specific questions such as "When did Columbus discover America?" are used, students use fewer words to answer them than to answer questions stating a relationship such as "Who came first, Marco Polo or Columbus?" Students used the most words to answer general questions such as "When did each of the following events occur?" Thus, specific, comparative, and general questions required increasingly more information for an answer. On the other hand, in a related experiment that allowed subjects a limited time to learn a text, subjects retained the least information when the text was preceded by general questions; they retained the most information with specific questions (Frase, 1969).

The Frase experiment showed that the nature of the question guides learning processes. General questions prompt a search of all the material, although they do not help students learn specifics; specific questions lead to specific answers, although they may allow the student to neglect general material. Each type of question has its advantages and disadvantages.

Before or after? When the question is asked also affects learning. Rothkopf (1966) examined the effects on comprehension of questions asked before and after the passage was read. He set up various groups that were given different combinations of questions (including no questions) before, during, and after reading a passage. After this, all groups were tested for comprehension.

Rothkopf found that using questions after reading doubled comprehension over using no questions. When answers were provided, comprehension was greater also. Students who had been told to pay careful attention to the passage had 10 or 15 percent better comprehension than a group that had been told only that it would be tested after reading the passage; even instructions to pay attention can affect mathemagenic activity. However, questions asked before reading improved comprehension only a little more than no questions.

A later study by Rothkopf and Bisbicos (1967) supported these conclusions and indicated that asking questions on textual material may help students maintain attention for longer periods of time. This study also asked students to recall certain kinds of information, such as places only versus technical names only; students appeared to focus only on the type of information asked for, ignoring other kinds of information. This finding suggests that test questions should be clearly related to the teacher's objectives. It also shows that specific questions asked before reading function like specific questions in general: they promote learning of the specific items to which they refer but inhibit general comprehension.

Questions asked after reading also increase the effectiveness of review statements (Bruning, 1968). In other words, while review statements alone increased learning, questions asked after reading further increased learning. Review and post-questions appear to have different functions. Review leads to acquisition of specific information tapped in the summary, while questions asked after reading increase the learning of general information.

Frequency of questions.   Many questions interspersed throughout textual material maintain an optimal level of learning behaviors. Questions motivate the learner to respond and provide him with feedback about his answer. Variations in frequency of questions seems to increase acquisition of general information rather than specific information. Probably most important, researchers assume that the frequent use of questions lets the learner confirm that he is using effective processing skills (Frase, 1970).

LANGUAGE IN
SOCIAL CONTEXT

CHAPTER
TEN
THE SOCIAL CONTEXTS
OF LANGUAGE

Since words refer to objects or events, we might expect all language communities to have equivalent words. Surprisingly, there are fewer than 100 equivalent items across all language communities. Furthermore, some communities have many meanings for the same word: *eye* might refer to the physiological organ of vision or it might mean *center*, as in "eye of a hurricane," "eye of round," or the "bull's-eye" of a target. Some communities have many words for something that has a single referent in another language community. For example, the Hanunoos have 90 words for rice, the Trobrianders have a dozen words for yams, the Eskimos have 20 different words for snow, and the Hopi Indians have one word for water in its natural state (as in lakes, streams, and waterfalls) and another word for water in containers. The Hopi Indians have a single word for all things that fly or are related to flying, including flying insects, airplanes, and pilots, while English-speaking people differentiate these objects. Similarly, people at different developmental levels will have different names for things. Young children tend to define objects in terms of actions: leaves are something you rake, bicycles are something you ride on, a ball is something you hit, and an orange is something you eat. Later, these descriptions expand to include features of the referent itself.

The meanings of words depend on the characteristics perceived by the observer in his speech community. Vocabulary differences among communities show different degrees of importance of an object or event to the members of those speech communities. Eskimos have 20 words for snow because they see snow in that many distinct ways.

We differentiate our immediate world of experience more finely than the world in general (Brown, 1965, p. 336). We notice many details about people who interest us and may remain oblivious to people who do not interest us. We name our pets and even our cars. We have a far greater vocabulary for subjects that interest us than for subjects that do not. If we choose to ignore certain aspects of reality, our perceptions may oblige us; the racist reveals that he makes only gross, not subtle, distinctions when he says, "They all look alike."

WHORF'S HYPOTHESIS

In contrast to the view that language *reflects* a community's view of the world, Whorf (1956) hypothesized that language *determines* the community's view of the world, or *Weltanschauung*. He claimed that differences among communities in speaking, perceiving, and thinking result from language rather than experience. It follows that perceptions in one language community would not be available to people in another language community.

Whorf's hypothesis is intriguing. It implies that communication among people in different language communities is difficult if not impossible. Words do have different referents, and only a few words are common to all language communities. Indeed, one often hears a speaker use a word from another language because there is no equivalent English word; examples are *Weltanschauung*, or one's view of, or orientation to, the world; *Gestalt*, or perceptual organizing characteristics or configuration; and *Einstellung*, or set.

Critics say Whorf's hypothesis is too limited—that language may *influence* thought processes but not determine them. More realistically, then, language differences probably indicate the different importance of certain objects in the environment; this may affect our ability to solve problems, to engage in other non-verbal behavior, or to form certain kinds of new concepts. Some attributes of an object or event necessarily supercede others in our experience and are given discriminatory labels. These attributes will then be more apparent than those with less specific labels. When it is necessary to identify these attributes before solving a problem, certain prior experiences and differentiations may be more helpful than others. Our language's words give us a handle for mentally manipulating a problem's variables. Without language, problem-solving activity would be hindered; similarly, some languages are better suited than other languages for solving some kinds of problems.

Although cultures differ in the way they code experiences, these differences are not absolute or irreversible. Contrary to Whorf, some observers feel that "the visual-verbal synesthetic relationships characteristic of our own language/culture community are shared by peoples who speak different languages and enjoy different cultures" (Osgood, 1960, p. 146). Furthermore, the people of any language community can learn other languages. Perhaps it would even be possible to create a common code that would fit all communities.

CONSEQUENCES OF
LANGUAGE DIFFERENCES

Dialects, or different speech patterns, occur in a language community. It is common to find variations in the pronunciation, vocabulary, or grammar of different groups of people using the language. Bostonians sometimes add an *r* to words ending in *a*, changing *Utica* into *Utiker*. *Root* rhymes with *put* in some parts of the country and with *jute* in others. The Pennsylvania Dutch say "When the little red car is, the train ain't," meaning "The caboose marks the end of the train," or "The train has gone by." The speech of some children sometimes combines many words into one giant word—for example, they might say "Uai-ga-na-ju" instead of "I ain't got no juice." Systematic differences in speech occur in different geographical regions (Northwestern, Eastern, Western, and Southern United States), cities in the same geographical region (Boston, Connecticut, and Philadelphia), ethnic groups (Polish, German, and Italian), races (white and black), and socioeconomic classes (middle and lower).

Dialects tend to acquire different levels of prestige. Standard English, for example, has the most prestige, whereas non-standard English has less prestige, depending on how far it departs from standard English. Blacks who live in the ghetto, Chicanos in the barrio, lower-class whites, or people with foreign origins may speak an English that is very different from the highly regarded standard English. The preference for standard English is not based on a desire to improve communication but on the fact that people who use standard English tend to have higher socioeconomic status than those who do not. The high status of foreign aristocrats' accents—which may be quite different from standard English—supports this point. This phenomenon occurs in other language communities as well.

NON-STANDARD ENGLISH:
DEFICIT OR DIFFERENCE?

There are two orientations toward non-standard English: the deficit model and the difference model.

The deficit model.   This model treats speech differences that deviate from the norm of middle-class whites as a serious limitation of one's ability to use the language in its presumably most powerful form (Engelmann, 1971). The pupil who misuses or omits words or fails to make complete sentences is assumed to be thinking illogically. To correct this deficiency, he must be given deliberate instruction to effect a change. Such instruction is guided by principles that define the deficit, the target behavior, the kinds of examples that should be presented to the learner, and the kinds of corrective feedback that should be used. This point of view holds that the deficit must be remedied by building necessary skills from the most basic of language elements.

The difference model. Another model holds that non-standard English is as much of a language system as standard English (Labov, 1969). A child who fails to use some words may not have a real deficiency: he may withhold these words in the presence of an authority (the experimenter) in self-defense because he perceives the language-production task to be threatening and hostile, as all other testing situations are for him. Such a child may use non-standard English forms that serve the same purpose as standard forms—for example, "He ain't got no book" means the same thing as "He has no book" (Wolfram, 1971). This model maintains that no variation of language is inferior or superior to any other variation. This model's instructional approaches are based on proceeding from the individual's language system to help the individual use his language efficiently.

Some conclusions. Carroll (1972) has stated the following conclusions about non-standard dialects. All languages have very similar forms that permit the expression of ideas, feelings, experiences, and thought. Languages clearly differ in their emphasis, their basic concepts, and their construction rules, yet they all are a means for communicating ideas related to time, space, number, and other variables. No language determines whether its users will think logically or illogically; languages are neutral in this respect and the characteristics of one's thinking ability are due more to individual differences than to language.

All languages have dialectal differences even among those called "standard." Speakers of the same dialect may change their style of speaking depending on whether the situation is formal, consultative, casual, or intimate, just as an individual would from one situation to another. All dialects in a language community are more or less intelligible, depending of course on their degree of similarity to the one used by the listener.

Differences in language competence (or the full knowledge the person has about such matters as vocabulary and grammatical rules) depend on ability, education, and the kind of exposure to other speakers of the language. But even speakers with the same degree of competence differ in their performance, or the way they actually use the language in speaking, reading, understanding, or writing. Furthermore, all children pass through similar developmental stages in learning the language. They learn the essential rules by the time they are 5 years old. However, they differ in how rapidly they proceed through the stages of development and in what they acquire during them; this depends on the level of maturation of their mental capacity and on exposure to meaningful learning situations.

Carroll's (1972) conclusions support the difference model. Although a non-standard speaker may appear to be inhibited in his speech or speak casually, leading to the conclusion that he is incapable of expressing ideas, his behavior may reflect his speaking style, which does not require him to formulate his thoughts carefully. Systematic omissions of words are found in many languages and are not considered deficiencies. Carroll mentions that black English omits the verb *to be* in such utterances as "He sick" and says that standard Russian does the same. Similarly, the double negative ("He ain't got no. . .") is used in black English as well as in Old English, French, and Spanish. Since these differences are not deficiencies, changing the child's language form, then, must be justified on other grounds—perhaps society's acceptance of one form over another or to teach the child new words or concepts that he has not learned in his own dialect.

Unfortunately, little research has examined the validity of the deficit model or the difference model.

The bicultural model.   Valentine (1971) has proposed a bicultural model that advocates dual socialization in both language forms since ethnic groups are committed both to their own culture and to the mainstream culture; he holds that the two cultures are not mutually exclusive. This model recognizes the "legitimacy and creativity of ethnic cultures [and that these cultures] are already more conversant with, and competent in, mainstream culture than most . . . believe or admit" (Valentine, 1971, p. 156). Valentine's model views variety within a culture as a positive characteristic that need not imply competitive alternatives.

STYLES OF SPEAKING: THE SOCIAL CONTEXT OF LINGUISTIC CODES IN COMMUNICATION

Linguistic codes are developed in the context of a culture. Bernstein (1970) distinguishes between two styles of speaking English—elaborated and restricted—which are used in either formal or informal situations, respectively. These styles are related to one's sub-culture, to his socialization, and to the degree of communication possible between speaker and listener. The differences between these two styles clarifies why some children from a lower-socioeconomic environment may meet difficulties in the middle-class school setting. Although the two styles will be discussed separately, no group uses one style exclusively.

The elaborated style. The elaborated style is developed in socialization patterns in which parents exercise linguistic control. Children receive explicit verbal instruction for acceptable and unacceptable behavior when critical incidents occur. These instructions take the form of rules accompanied by general principles, reasons, and explanations. With increasing experience, the child can generalize these rules to other situations. At the same time, he learns to understand and speak with a diversified vocabulary in more or less carefully constructed sentences.

The elaborated style uses a variety of syntactic alternatives, adverbs and adjectives, prepositions, alternate phrases for the same meaning, and verbal qualifications of meaning. The speaker's intent is to make his communication as clear as possible. It reflects careful planning in which the listener's interpretation is not taken for granted. Sometimes, when meanings are elaborated, the speaker will borrow from the listener's experience to make the spoken meaning explicit.

The elaborated style is based almost exclusively on verbal channels rather than extraverbal channels (gestures, pointing, facial expressions) or a mix of the two. It is a highly adaptive and flexible means of conveying information and offers a greater range of alternatives for expressing one's ideas than communication based on vague verbalizations or gestures. Accordingly, it facilitates the communication of individualized meanings and encourages the expression of novel meanings and complex organizations of meanings (concepts, principles, taxonomies). The child reared with this speaking style is at an advantage: he can actively seek out and extend meanings, and he has available the verbal means for resolving ambiguity.

The restricted style. The restricted style is also learned through access to social roles in the family, peer group, school, and work situations. Bernstein (1970) indicates that in its most extreme form, its syntactical alternatives are restricted or limited.

A community in which the restricted style prevails assumes that the child can be controlled by emphasis on specific behavioral situations rather than by instructions that lead to the formation of general or universal rules. The child certainly learns whether others approve or disapprove of his actions, but here the similarity between the two styles presumably ends. The restricted style is characterized by rapid, fluent speech in which words are often run together; informational sequences are sometimes disconnected and dislocated, reflecting a lack of planning, a small vocabulary, poor syntactical form, and limited and restricted use of conjunctions, adjectives, and adverbs. Control is not accompanied by explanation, reason, or anticipation of consequences. For example, the child might be told to "Stop it!" If he asks why, the answer might be, "Don't make such a fuss, it's just not right." Such admonitions may result in guilt (the child feels he is at fault for some reason unknown to him), the child's curiosity may be inhibited, his orientation may become directed toward the immediate consequences of a given behavior rather than longer-range consequences, and his sensitivity to parental or other authority may be increased at the expense of independence.

The restricted style is implicit while the elaborated style is explicit. This characteristic is most apparent in interactions in which experiences are closely shared by participants. For example, a telephone conversation between two adolescents often uses the restrictive style extremely fluently. Their conversation will be verbose and vague, with abbreviated sentences, personal references, and frequent jumping from one topic to another. Their meanings may be perfectly clear to each other but not as clear to an observer such as a parent who does not share the same experiences. Shared experiences, identifications, and loyalties remove the necessity for elaborating meaning or providing logical continuity. Often such speakers continually interject "You know what I mean." The restricted style depends more on gestures, shifts in intonation, references to earlier experiences or conversations, and facial expressions to convey the intended meaning. Although the restricted style can convey meaning, it does not have the same capacity for generating new meanings as does the elaborated style.

Again, all speakers use both styles of speaking. The lower-class speaker may use an informal style with his peers but will change to a more formal style when interacting in formal situations such as reading aloud or talking to his employer. A teacher may use the elaborated style in the classroom but may use the restricted style when speaking with another teacher. A husband and wife may convey as much by a gesture or a comment in the restricted style as by much more complex verbal elaborations.

The two styles reflect the way a language community communicates in a given social context. A child who has learned only the informal style will be at a disadvantage in school, where the tendency is to use the formal style. Apparent rather than real differences in IQ, inability to deal with abstract concepts, language difficulties, and inability to profit from school may result from using the informal style exclusively since the pupil may feel that his intent is clear when it is not (Bernstein, 1970, p. 37, for example). Teachers should recognize that people do differ in the way they express their intent, yet a child who is limited to the informal style may be handicapped in school and certain work situations. Although the informal style should be viewed as an indicator of performance rather than competence, the pupil should be taught, as sensitively as possible, to use the elaborated style.

THE SOCIAL IMPORTANCE OF
LANGUAGE DIFFERENCES

However different non-standard English appears from standard English, both are highly structured systems. Both can convey the base meanings although surface meanings may differ. Non-standard English is more interesting than it may seem to the casual observer. Labov (1969) illustrates this by describing the original and ingenious ways language is used in the game "Dozens," which consists of a rapid exchange of insults requiring well-developed verbal skills. The richly elaborated and embellished toasts and jokes that are part of the oratorical repertoire of many users of non-standard English also indicate its wealth of nuance. Although standard English uses longer sentences, has a larger vocabulary, is richer in impersonal evaluative statements, and excels in taking the role of the generalized other compared to non-standard English, there is no clear evidence how much of these differences are functional (Labov, 1969).

The social meanings of accented English.   When learning language, the child learns its social meanings, including the social meanings of accented speech. An English accent is more authoritative than a Southern accent. Middle-class language patterns convey more prestige than lower-class language patterns. The formal style is valued more highly than the informal style, and standard English is valued more highly than non-standard forms. All social groups in our society place similar values on these forms. Politicians, leaders, and writers do not use the vernacular, although there is a greater tendency to do so today than formerly. The following jobs show a range of from great likelihood that the formal style will be used to little likelihood that the formal style will be used: television announcer, teacher, office manager, postal clerk, foreman, factory worker (Labov, 1969).

Evaluations of different styles.   In highly stratified situations, the dominant group's values regarding the language system are held by all. For example, Lambert (1967) says that the Quebec community values English more highly than Canadian French. When the same person addresses groups of English Canadians in English he is rated as more personable, intelligent, dependable, ambitious, and taller than when he uses Canadian French. Surprisingly, the French-Canadians do not rate him in the opposite way. They make the same ratings. People in the United States tend to do the same when comparing standard English to their own vernacular forms. Furthermore, "Those who have the highest degree of a stigmatized form in their casual speech are quickest to stigmatize it in the speech of others" (Labov, 1969, p. 29).

Style shifting. Social evaluation of language styles results in people changing their speaking style for different situations. New Yorkers from different socioeconomic classes differ greatly in their use of /th/ and /ing/. When using casual speech, members of the lower class pronounce /th/ as /t/ and /ing/ as /in/—for example, *three* becomes *tree*, *thing* becomes *ting*, and *working* becomes *workin*—more often than does the speaker in the lower-middle or upper-middle class. However, all groups shift to a more formal pronunciation (the standard pronunciation of /th/ and /ing/) when using careful speech or when reading isolated words.

Labov also observes that teen-agers use formal speech patterns in school but among their peers or at home they shift to the vernacular. Women show greater shifts in style than men; although they react strongly against the vernacular form of the language, they tend to use it more in casual speech but become more meticulous in formal speech than do men.

Older children are more sensitive to style differences than are younger children. Although the young child may see the difference, he may not be aware of its significance. One 12-year-old's responses were:

> "Have you ever heard anyone say *dese, dat,* and *dose?*"
> "Un-huh."
> "What kind of person says that?"
> "I don't know" [Labov, 1969, p. 33].

While style shifts do occur in predictable situations, the more formal styles may break down under conditions of stress or complete relaxation, at which time one reverts to the form most commonly used in casual speech—that is, the basic vernacular learned before 13 or 14 years of age.

In summary, style shifting is due to social evaluation. Formal style requires greater attention to vocabulary and syntax so as to approximate the norm of the television announcer or newspaper columnist. Informal style permits less emphasis on pronunciation and permits use of the vernacular. Individuals shift between these two styles according to the situation they are in. Bilinguals shift more in their native language than in their acquired language, in which they may know only the formal style.

IMPLICATIONS OF SOCIAL MEANINGS OF LANGUAGE FOR TEACHING

The child who uses non-standard English may not be able to change from non-standard to standard English easily. In this case, the teacher can demonstrate. There are, after all, alternate forms for "He don't know nothing" ("He doesn't know anything"), "Nobody don't like him" ("Nobody likes him"), or "Nobody can't do it" ("Nobody can do it"). All of these involve the same rule (that is, the negative is attracted *only* to the first indefinite) which can be used to express a number of alternative ideas (Labov, 1969, p. 8). With this understanding, the teacher can safely assume that the pupil's rules are not the same as his own. Obviously, teaching the formal rule that is confusing even to adults would not help. However, by feedback and correction, the teacher effects a change by providing examples that build on something the child knows together with whatever contrasts and explanations are necessary. This enables the pupil to understand how his system differs from the teacher's and why changes must be made.

Too often, the teacher's demands in language instruction—whether in speaking, writing, or reading—are unrealistic. Required changes often force the non-standard speaker into conflict with his peer culture. Language patterns, including dialects, stem from loyalty to the culture in which they were acquired. To regard some differences as sloppy or illiterate is to ignore their value to the speaker and to cast aspersions on the pupil's culture. Often, such appraisals may be made inadvertently, as when the child is forced to hear and say the different sounds in *pin* and *pen*. In such cases, this may be an unreasonable requirement, especially since the child may be unable to hear the difference. (When the vowels *i* and *e* are followed by *m* or *n* they often do sound the same to many listeners.) This demand, too strongly made, may lead to direct, destructive conflict between teacher and pupil.

Furthermore, persons who use the vernacular are the ones most likely to denounce its use by others. This group includes more women than men and teachers who come from backgrounds similar to their pupils' backgrounds. They perceive the difference in language usage more easily than other teachers might, but at the same time they have a more extreme reaction to this difference. Such teachers need to be sensitive to this fact and must try to temper their reactions.

Differences in language usage may cause still other conflicts. For example, the non-standard speaker may not have the same rules for politeness as standard speakers do (Labov, 1969). The pupil from the ghetto may forthrightly say "You lie!" to a teacher who has differed with him, while a middle-class child might say "There is another way of looking at this problem" or "There is my side of the story." On this basis, the middle-class pupil is often considered polite, and the lower-class pupil is considered defiant, aggressive, and hostile. Labov (1969) cites cases of boys who had been severely reprimanded or demoted mainly because their codes did not include accepted rules for politeness (p. 53). Of course, some expressions of hostility may be just that—hostility—but they may also be expressions constructed from syntax that fails to include socially acceptable ways of objecting or refusing.

The academic performance of the pupil who is a non-standard speaker may suffer. When responding in class or in testing situations, such pupils may find it difficult to make themselves understood by the middle-class teacher; they may be inhibited from talking at all and be regarded as lacking in ability. Yet in their peer group, such children's communication may be efficient and effective. Reading ability and expression by lower-class and middle-class children are equalized when the lower-class child uses materials that are adapted to his form of the language. But, the adverse effects of authority relationships, which place the child in a subordinate role, become compounded when combined with the effects of different language styles that hinder understanding. Children from the lower class or ghetto are at an unjustifiable disadvantage in such educational settings.

Labov and other advocates of the linguistic difference model have suggested that at least some of the problems in reading, in testing situations, and in encouraging children to express themselves can be overcome by using the vernacular in initial contacts and then providing instruction on changes that should be made. Some students of black English (for example, Stewart, 1969) have suggested that the use of vernacular primers will solve structural problems of grammatical interference between the child's dialect and the standard language; on the other hand, Labov believes that the primary value of such primers would be to overcome the cultural and social conflict in the classroom if they can be seen and approved by the community as the best means of transition to reading and writing in the standard language.

CHAPTER ELEVEN
LEARNING ANOTHER LANGUAGE

When one is exposed to a language other than his native language, he ordinarily acquires a certain degree of competence in the second language (*bilingualism*). At one extreme, the person may become equally fluent in reading, writing, and understanding both languages; at the other extreme, he may be able only to speak and understand his native language but not read it and only to understand but not speak, read, or write the second language.

DEGREES OF BILINGUALISM

Bilingual individuals can vary considerably in their mastery of phonemes and graphemes in speaking or writing, vocabulary, semantics, and syntax in either language. These differences in degree of bilingualism can be measured in several ways (Macnamara, 1967). (1) Fluency is measured by how long it takes one to name pictures or follow simple instructions in each of the two languages. Fluency has also been measured by the number of words produced in either language in response to the stimulus of a given letter or pairs of letters. (2) Tests to measure the dominance of one language over the other require the person to respond to an ambiguous written word that properly belongs in both languages but is interpreted or pronounced differently in each one. The language most frequently used in such responses is considered the dominant one. Scores from these tests tend to correlate with each other, with the individual's self-ratings of his skill in the two languages, and with the degree to which he uses each language.

COORDINATE AND COMPOUND BILINGUALS

There are two kinds of bilinguals. The compound bilingual uses the same meanings for corresponding words in both languages; this occurs when both languages were learned in the same setting (for example, in a bilingual home). The coordinate bilingual tends to apply different meanings to corresponding words in the two languages; in such cases, each language was probably learned in a different setting (for example, German in Germany and English in Canada).

The behavioral consequences of the distinction between coordinate and compound bilingualism have been demonstrated in a limited way by Lambert and Jakobovits (1960). They extinguished the tone, or connotative meaning, of words through satiation, a procedure in which the speaker repeats a word several times. (Try it yourself: repeat a particularly offensive word rapidly for a minute or two and note whether the tone of the word seems to change.) Compound bilinguals satiated only on words in one language were found to be also satiated on corresponding words in the other language. Coordinate bilinguals satiated on words in one language were not. Thus, for compound bilinguals, equivalent words in both languages seem to be actually equivalent. For the coordinate bilinguals, connotative meanings are not as readily transferred from one language to the other.

Differences between the two groups have not been so clearly defined in parallel studies that considered denotative meanings. As Macnamara (1967) cautions, failure to identify differences between coordinates and compounds in performance in satiation tasks is not necessarily conclusive since most studies have been conducted with single words in isolation, whereas language communication depends on the total context in which a word appears. In typical discourse, we might expect clearer differentiations between the two kinds of bilinguals.

BILINGUALISM AND THINKING

The distinction between coordinate and compound bilinguals suggests that if bilinguals and monolinguals differ in their thinking behavior, it may be due to the way the two languages were learned or are used rather than merely because of bilingualism. For example, switching from one language to the other and translating meanings from one language to the other may cause interference. Consequently, bilingualism may affect thinking ability in other ways than those suggested by the compound-coordinate distinction.

An anecdote. Haugen (1956) cites interesting anecdotal evidence:

> Lowie was one of those who retained his German while learning English and sought to develop both of them into adequate creative instruments. In his summing up he writes: "I am impressed with the difficulty of mastering a single language, let alone two languages, in the fullest sense. . . . [The bilingual] suffers in either tongue when judged by the highest standards . . . but he also has insights not granted in quite so vivid a manner to others. . . . The popular impression that a man alters his personality when speaking

another tongue is far from ill-grounded. When I speak German to Germans, I automatically shift my orientation as a social being." The French-born American writer Julian Green has also told of the problems involved in being a bilingual writer. He writes, "I am more and more inclined to believe that it is almost an impossibility to be absolutely bilingual." He tells of his attempt to translate one of his own books from French to English: it failed, and he had to sit down and write an entirely new book: "It was as if, writing in English, I had become another person* [Haugen, 1956, pp. 69–70].

In an experiment comparing the learning of two artificial vocabularies (Yeni-Komshian & Lambert, 1969), concurrent learning (comparable to learning by compound bilinguals) and consecutive learning (comparable to learning by coordinate bilinguals) were compared. Initially, the concurrent group experienced more interference than did the consecutive group, thus providing some evidence for the kind of interference expressed in the preceding anecdotes.

Creativity.   Bilingualism has been linked with creativity, at least on the basis of anecdotal evidence. The ability to think in two languages is sometimes assumed to permit greater variation in responses, one of the conditions for creativity. This speculation has been countered by others who suggest bilinguals can never become great scholars or authors because of the limitations of interference from such factors as dual translation and switching. However, the many scholars who are fluent bilinguals and multilinguals leads one to discount this argument.

Intelligence.   The frequently heard assertion that bilinguals are more subject to stuttering or have low intelligence (as measured by intelligence tests) also seems questionable. Any differences are more likely to result from associated factors than from bilingualism itself. For example, bilinguals who learned the language of the intelligence test in their early childhood years perform about two years below average on the verbal part of the intelligence test. However, on the non-verbal part, they function about the same as the average child does. Thus, the bilingual child may perform more poorly on such tests than does his monolingual counterpart because he is less familiar with the test language. Some of the difference may also be due to handicaps imposed by the social environment. As socioeconomic environmental conditions become more similar, differences in test performance decrease. Peal and Lambert (1962) found that bilingual children in Montreal scored higher on intelligence tests than did their monolingual counterparts.

*From Haugen, E. *Bilingualism in the Americas: A Bibliography and Research Guide.* American Dialect Society Publication No. 26. Copyright 1956 The American Dialect Society. Reprinted by permission of The American Dialect Society and the University of Alabama Press.

Furthermore, they concluded that the balanced bilingual (one who has equal facility in two languages) has an advantage in terms of cognitive flexibility, conceptualization, and diversification of cognitive abilities.

SOCIAL CONSEQUENCES OF BILINGUALISM

Conflicts may be created in the home when children bring the language taught in the school to the home, where another language is spoken. One Italian-American woman raised in such circumstances said, "My mother took no notice of such childish snobbery. As long as I remained under her jurisdiction she continued to cling to her policy of restricting the family language to Italian. [She said,] 'I might as well not have children if I can't talk to them' " (Haugen, 1956, p. 70).

SOCIAL MOBILITY AND BILINGUALISM

People who are somewhat uncertain about their societal role reflect this insecurity by switching (in pronunciation, intonation, use of words, or syntax) between the two languages more frequently than do more secure individuals. Ervin and Osgood (1954) point out the importance of psychosocial factors in learning the second language. They note that young children seek membership in peer groups and are motivated to learn both languages. On the other hand, adolescents lack the motivation to adapt to a new norm, which is required to learn a new language.

Diebold (1964) described the social factors in learning a second language in natural settings. In a study of a relatively isolated Mexican group, he found that Huave Indians who desired to move upward to the Mestizo (high-prestige) group had to learn Spanish, which was not their native language. However, social factors sometimes interfered with the process. The new dominant language had to be learned outside of the home, but the primary sources of the second language were the Spanish-speaking merchants, who did not learn the language of the Huave Indians, and who kept the Huave at a disadvantage in order to maintain their power. Accordingly, one finds that the Huave Indians borrowed dominant words from Spanish but the Spanish-speaking merchants did not borrow words from the Huave Indians' language. Consequently, few, if any, models of the dominant language enjoyed prestige and at the same time had the communicator roles that could integrate the two languages. Those who spoke both languages spoke the Huave Indians' language only with some embarrassment.

Today, the dominant Spanish language is being incorporated into the Indian language in the form of *loan words*. The word *àsét* (for *oil*) is borrowed from the Spanish *asceite*, and *nimàl* (for *animal*) is borrowed from the Spanish *animal*. Diebold found little evidence for interference in the opposite direction. In this illustration, then, we see evidence of the way language can be used to maintain political dependence by the more prestigious group as well as of languages in transition.

LOYALTY TO ONE'S CULTURE AND BILINGUALISM

Adherence to one's native language or dialect symbolizes identity and loyalty to one's culture. French-Canadians may feel it unnecessary to learn English; if they do learn English, they might not use it since to do so symbolizes relinquishing some of their cherished values. Similar relationships exist where racial, socioeconomic, regional, or ethnic groups adhere to their native dialects or languages. We have all met people who take pride in using a native foreign language or in maintaining their British or Southern accent. People often feel that their native language identifies them with masculinity, with their family or culture, or with prestige. Accordingly, change and the motivation to learn either standard English or a new language comes slowly since it is incompatible with these attitudes. When a new language is learned, it is for practical reasons, such as better chances to find work. Pleasant circumstances in which there have been no feelings of self-rejection, social rejection, or antagonism contribute to the desire of the person to learn and use the new language (Haugen, 1956).

The feelings associated with demands to change to standard English as a second language are well illustrated in this passage about Mexican children:

> School is where it starts, and school can be a frightful experience for most Chicano children. It was for me. The subtle prejudice and the not-so-subtle arrogance of Anglos came at me at a very early age, although it took many years to realize and comprehend what took place. The SPEAK ENGLISH signs in every hall and doorway and the unmitigated efforts of the Anglo teachers to eradicate the Spanish language, coupled with their demands for behavioral changes, clearly pointed out to me that I was not acceptable. . . . The association between being different and being inferior was quite difficult to resist, and it tortured me for many years [Gomez, 1968, pp. 8–9; in John & Horner, 1970, p. 144].

LEARNING A SECOND LANGUAGE

The emotional, political, social, and educational factors involved in learning through a second language may inflict emotional and intellectual damage. John and Horner (1970) have suggested the desirability of bilingual teaching although they recognize that research on the social implications of such methods is scant. However, they suggest that, with appropriate cautions, a bilingual approach for teaching children who would otherwise have to relinquish their native language in an English-speaking educational system is pedagogically sound.

ENGLISH AS A SECOND LANGUAGE: A BILINGUAL APPROACH

In an experiment in the Phillipines, described briefly by John and Horner (1970), one group of children was taught initially in the mother tongue for the first two grades while learning English and then switched to instruction in English. A control group was taught in the traditional way—in English throughout. After about two months, the performance of the experimental group surpassed that of the control group in all tested subjects as well as in the use of English. Similar results were obtained in experimental programs in Sweden, Mexico, Miami, and San Antonio. In some of these experiments, improved social and emotional adjustments of children in the experimental group were noted.

In view of the demands on the child during his period of early cognitive growth that occurs in the first years in school, John and Horner's (1970) position seems sensible and reasonable. The child's cognitive ability is helped by language, but he also has primitive capacities for conceptualization that do not depend on language. In the early elementary grades, language learning accelerates; many new words and complex sentence constructions as well as new skills and attitudes must be learned. Unfortunately, the child who does not speak standard English must accomplish these feats of thinking and problem-solving in a language that is foreign to him.

Education based on a bilingual approach certainly has the advantage of permitting the child to acquire initial habits of thinking with language at the time such skills are emerging during the concrete operations period. Once these skills have been acquired, they can be used to acquire a second language. Next, the second language can be used to extend the pupil's language skill (John & Horner, 1970).

LEARNING A SECOND LANGUAGE IN SCHOOL

So far, Chapter Eleven has discussed pupils who learn a second language in more or less natural conditions or under social, economic, or political pressures. Some come from homes in which both languages are spoken. Others come from homes in which only one language is spoken and they must then learn a second language in order to adapt to a given educational or social system.

A place in the curriculum.   However, some educators believe that learning a foreign language is as desirable an objective as learning mathematics or chemistry. Accordingly, some elementary schools teach foreign languages, as do high schools and colleges; at one time, competence in a foreign language or two was required of all Ph.D. candidates. While the compound bilingual sometimes learns the two languages simultaneously, the new language is usually learned in school as a second language. It is built on knowledge of the first language and so is different in many respects from first-language learning.

Does the young child learn a second language more easily than the older child? It is commonly believed that he does, and anecdotal evidence indicates that 2- or 3-year-olds can attain competence, for their age level, in two languages quite easily. When the indigenous language is learned by a non-native adult speaker, he sometimes seems to lack full competence either in vocabulary, pronunciation, or syntax.

How long does it take to learn a second language? Carroll (1969) reports that an adult receiving intensive training in foreign language requires 250 to 500 hours of training to achieve a comfortable level of fluency. It is difficult to test whether children and adults learn a second language at different rates, since children learn, in general, at a different rate than adults, and their backgrounds in language when they begin to learn the second language are at different levels from adults. Their motivations differ from those of adults. Their interests differ. These factors affect the kinds of teaching techniques and reading materials that can be used. However, children do learn to pronounce words more easily than adults; this may explain why casual observation suggests that children learn a second language more easily than do adults. On the other hand, children and adults learn grammar at about the same rate, but adults learn vocabulary items more rapidly than children do.

Some benefits of learning a second language.   Since a second language requires much time to learn, practical considerations encourage teaching the second language at an early age if a second language is needed. Greater competence in the second language seems to result from learning it at an early age, although this may be due to the longer time spent learning the language in comparison with the shorter time spent if it is first learned in secondary school and the even shorter time spent if it is initially learned in college. Carroll argues that time spent is an important variable in learning the second language. Although the evidence is not clear on whether early learning of a second language facilitates its relearning at a later time, one would expect from our knowledge of transfer that there should be such facilitative effects.

Benefits from learning a second language extend beyond the classroom. With the current emphasis on travel in our modern society, with the number of foreign films now being shown, with the easy availability of foreign newspapers, and with the contact today's students have with people of other cultures, young pupils will benefit from learning a modern foreign language. Most students will be able to practice their foreign language outside of school.

Learning a second language is sometimes said to facilitate learning other languages. Some evidence suggests that those who learn a second language easily may have greater aptitude for learning any language. Differences in language aptitude appear when the child is 9 or 10 years old. When there is positive transfer, it is between similar languages such as Spanish, Portuguese, and Italian but not between dissimilar languages such as romance languages and Russian or Chinese. This suggests that skills and processes rather than content may be what is transferred. Accordingly, similarities or differences in the way the languages are constructed should be given some consideration in curriculum planning.

A FIELD STUDY ON
TEACHING A SECOND LANGUAGE

Only a few experimental field studies have examined the consequences of learning a second language on the pupil's other achievements. However, a carefully conducted study by Lambert and Macnamara (1969) illustrates how this might be accomplished. Their study was conducted in Montreal where French and English bilingualism is important socially and politically. English-speaking children in that city can easily become bilingual if they have the opportunity to interact regularly with those who speak French. In fact, there has been considerable motivation for doing so; for example, the non-French speakers now living in Quebec find increasingly stronger socioeconomic pressures to learn French than they did formerly.

Lambert and Macnamara assigned a group of first-grade English-speaking children (experimental group) to an all-French school, where they were taught by the same methods and in the same language as all other children in the school. The performance of the experimental group was compared with that of French-speaking children in another all-French school (French controls) and with English-speaking children in all-English schools (English controls). Both control groups were in neighborhoods similar to that of the experimental group. There was also a companion French-speaking control group in the same school in which the experimental group was placed. All groups were equated on intelligence and socio-economic indices.

After one year, the performance of pupils in the experimental class was slightly below that of pupils in the English control group, but the English-speaking skills of pupils in the experimental group were still in the 50th percentile, and their English reading skills were at the 15th percentile, according to American norms. Pupils in the experimental class had no difficulty comprehending or speaking English although they made more errors and had a slower output of words relative to their English-taught controls. Responses to word-association tests were equally rapid in both groups. However, pupils in the experimental class gave more common, less imaginative answers than their counterparts in the English-taught control group. Nevertheless, the experimental group showed good progress in French and showed average performance (compared to native speakers) in producing basic sound units. In the passive aspects of French (tests of word discrimination, sentence comprehension, and word order), the experimental subjects were as creative and flexible as their French controls. They were better than the French controls in ability to associate the sound and spelling of French words—the experimental group had learned quite a lot about how to process French words. In mathematics, they did as well as both French and English controls. There was no evidence that the experiment's training contributed to more sensitivity in differentiating new linguistic sounds or to greater cognitive or mental flexibility. Other experiments must test the permanency of these effects, but this study is a prototype for other studies in this very important aspect of language learning.

REFERENCES

Anisfeld, M., & Gordon, M. On the psychophonological structure of English inflectional rules. *Journal of Verbal Learning and Verbal Behavior,* 1968, **7**, 973–979.

Ausubel, D. *Educational psychology: A cognitive view.* New York: Holt, Rinehart & Winston, 1968.

Ausubel, D. P., & Fitzgerald, D. Organizer, general background, and antecedent learning variables in sequential verbal learning. *Journal of Educational Psychology,* 1962, **53**, 243–249.

Baratz, J. C. Teaching reading in an urban Negro school system. In J. C. Baratz & R. W. Shuy (Eds.), *Teaching black children to read.* Washington, D. C.: Center for Applied Linguistics, 1969.

Bartlett, F. C. *Remembering: A study in experimental and social psychology.* Cambridge, England: University Press, 1932.

Bereiter, C., & Engelmann, S. *Teaching disadvantaged children in the pre-school.* Englewood Cliffs, N. J.: Prentice-Hall, 1966.

Berko, J. The child's learning of English morphology. *Word,* 1958, **14**, 150–177.

Bernstein, B. A sociolinguistic approach to socialization with some reference to educability. In F. Williams (Ed.), *Language and poverty: Perspectives on a theme.* Chicago: Markham, 1970.

Betts, E. A. Ride in. In *Time to play,* 3rd ed., second pre-primer, Betts Basic Readers, Language Art Series. New York: American Book, 1963.

Betts, E. A., & Welch, C. M. Stop and go. In *All in a day,* third pre-primer, Betts Basic Readers. New York: American Book, 1963.

Bever, T. G. The cognitive basis for linguistic structures. In J. R. Hayes (Ed.), *Cognition and the development of language.* New York: Wiley, 1970.

Bloom, L. *Language development: Form and function in emerging grammars.* Cambridge: Massachusetts Institute of Technology Press, 1970.

Bourne, L. E., Jr. Learning and utilization of conceptual rules. In B. Kleinmuntz (Ed.), *Concepts and the structure of memory.* New York: Wiley, 1967.

Bousfield, W. A. The occurrence of clustering in recall of randomly assigned associates. *Journal of General Psychology,* 1953, **49**, 229–273.

Bower, G. H. Analysis of a mnemonic device. *American Scientist,* 1970, **58**, 496–510.

Bower, G. H. A selective review of organizational factors in memory. In E. Tulving & W. Donaldson (Eds.), *Organization of memory.* New York: Academic Press, 1972.

Bower, G. H., Clark, M., Lesgold, A. M., & Winzenz, D. Hierarchical retrieval schemes in recall of categorical word lists. *Journal of Verbal Learning and Verbal Behavior,* 1969, **8**, 323–343.

Braine, M. D. S. The ontogeny of English phrase structure: The first phase. *Language,* 1963, **39**, 1–13.

Bransford, J. D., Barclay, J. R., & Franks, J. J. Sentence memory: A constructive versus interpretive approach. *Cognitive Psychology*, 1972, **3**, 193–209.

Bransford, J. D., & Franks, J. J. Temporal integration in the acquisition of complex linguistic ideas. In J. J. Jenkins (Chairman), *Understanding sentences*. Symposium presented at the Midwestern Psychological Association, Cincinnati, May, 1970.

Bransford, J. D., & Franks, J. J. The abstraction of linguistic ideas. *Cognitive Psychology*, 1971, **2**, 331–350.

Bransford, J. D., & Johnson, M. K. Conceptual prerequisites for understanding: Some investigations of comprehension and recall. *Journal of Verbal Learning and Verbal Behavior*, 1972, **11**, 717–726.

Brown, R. *Social psychology*. New York: Free Press, 1965.

Brown, R. Development of the first language in the human species. *American Psychologist*, 1973, **28**, 97–106. (a)

Brown, R. *A first language: The early stages*. Cambridge: Harvard University Press, 1973. (b)

Brown, R., & Bellugi, U. Three processes in the child's acquisition of syntax. *Harvard Educational Review*, 1964, **34**, 133–151.

Brown, R., & Fraser, C. The acquisition of syntax. In C. N. Cofer & B. S. Musgrave (Eds.), *Verbal behavior and learning: Problems and processes*. New York: McGraw-Hill, 1963.

Brown, R., & Fraser, C. The acquisition of syntax. *Monograph of the Society for Research in Child Development*, 1964, **29**(1), 43–79.

Brown, R., & Hanlon, C. Derivational complexity and order of acquisition in child speech. In J. R. Hayes (Ed.), *Cognition and the development of language*. New York: Wiley, 1970.

Brown, R., & McNeill, D. The "tip-of-the-tongue" phenomenon. *Journal of Verbal Learning and Verbal Behavior*, 1966, **5**, 325–337.

Bruner, J. S. The course of cognitive growth. *American Psychologist*, 1964, **19**, 1–15.

Bruner, J. S., & Minturn, A. L. Perceptual identification and perceptual organization. *Journal of Genetic Psychology*, 1955, **53**, 21–28.

Bruner, J. S., & Olver, R. R. The development of equivalence transformations in children. *Monographs of the Society for Research in Child Development*, 1963, **28**(2), serial no. 86.

Bruner, J. S., Olver, R. R., & Greenfield, P. *Studies in cognitive growth*. New York: Wiley, 1966.

Bruning, R. H. Effects of review and test-like events within the learning of prose materials. *Journal of Educational Psychology*, 1968, **59**, 16–19.

Campos, N., & Radecki, W. Experimental investigation into the influence of forgotten mnemonic material on voluntary association. *ANAIS da Colonia de Psychopathas*, 1928, **1**, 219–243.

Carroll, J. B. Psychological and educational research into second language teaching to young children. In H. H. Stern (Ed.), *Languages and the young school child*. London: Oxford University Press, 1969.

Carroll, J. B. Language and cognition. In J. F. Rosenblith, W. Allinsmith, & J. P. Williams (Eds.), *The causes of behavior*, 3rd ed. Boston: Allyn & Bacon, 1972.

Carson, R. L. *The sea around us*, rev. ed. New York: Oxford University Press, 1961.

Chomsky, C. *The acquisition of syntax in children from 5 to 10*. Research Monograph No. 57. Cambridge: Massachusetts Institute of Technology Press, 1969.

Chomsky, N. *Syntactic structures*. The Hague: Mouton & Co., 1957.

Chomsky, N. Review of Skinner's *Verbal behavior*. *Language*, 1959, **35**, 26–58.

Chomsky, N. Comments for Project Literacy meeting. *Project Literacy Reports*, 1964, no. 2.

Chomsky, N. *Aspects of the theory of language*. Cambridge: Massachusetts Institute of Technology Press, 1965.

Clark, H. H., & Clark, E. V. Semantic distinctions and memory for complex sentences. *Quarterly Journal of Experimental Psychology*, 1968, **20**, 129–138.

Cofer, C. N. Verbal behavior in relation to reasoning and values. In H. Guetzkow (Ed.), *Groups, leadership, and men*. Pittsburgh: Carnegie Press, 1951.

Cofer, C. N. Reasoning as an associative process: III. The role of verbal responses in problem solving. *Journal of General Psychology*, 1957, **57**, 55–68.

Collins, A. M., & Quillian, M. R. How to make a language user. In E. Tulving & W. Donaldson (Eds.), *Organization of memory*. New York: Academic Press, 1972.

Dember, W. N., & Jenkins, J. J. *General psychology: Modeling behavior and experience*. Englewood Cliffs, N. J.: Prentice-Hall, 1970.

de Selincourt, A., Trans. *Herodotus: The histories*. London: Penguin, 1964.

Diebold, A. R., Jr. Incipient bilingualism. In D. Hymes (Ed.), *Language in culture and society: A reader in linguistics and anthropology*. New York: Harper & Row, 1964.

DiVesta, F. J., & Rickards, J. P. Effects of labeling and articulation on the attainment of concrete, abstract, and number concepts. *Journal of Experimental Psychology*, 1971, **88**, 41–49.

Di Vesta, F. J., & Walls, R. T. A factor analysis of the semantic attributes of 487 words and some relationships to the conceptual behavior of fifth-grade children. *Journal of Educational Psychology Monograph*, 1970, **61**(2), whole no. 6.

Donaldson, M., & Balfour, G. Less is more: A study of language comprehension in children. *British Journal of Psychology*, 1968, **59**, 461–471.

Ebbinghaus, H. *Uber das Gedächtnis: Untersuchungen zur experimentellen Psychologie*. Leipzig: Duncker & Humblot, 1885. H. A. Ruger & C. E. Bussenius, Trans., *Memory: A contribution to experimental psychology*. New York: Teachers College, Columbia University, Bureau of Publications, 1913.

Engelmann, S. The inadequacies of the linguistic approach in teaching situations. In R. W. Shuy (Ed.), *Sociolinguistics: A cross-disciplinary approach*. Washington, D. C.: Center for Applied Linguistics, 1971.

Ervin, S. M. Imitation and structural change in children's language. In E. Lenneberg (Ed.), *New directions in the study of language*. Cambridge: Massachusetts Institute of Technology Press, 1961.

Ervin, S. M., & Foster, G. The development of meaning in children's descriptive terms. *Journal of Abnormal Social Psychology*, 1960, **61**, 271–275.

Ervin, S. M., & Osgood, C. E. Second language learning and bilingualism. *Journal of Abnormal and Social Psychology*, 1954, **49**, 139–146.

Faust, G. W., & Anderson, R. C. Effects of incidental material in a programmed Russian vocabulary lesson. *Journal of Educational Psychology*, 1967, **58**, 3–10.

Fillmore, C. J. The case for case. In E. Bach & R. T. Harms (Eds.), *Universals in linguistic theory*. New York: Holt, Rinehart & Winston, 1968.

Fodor, J. A., & Bever, T. G. The psychological reality of linguistic segments. *Journal of Verbal Learning and Verbal Behavior*, 1965, **4**, 414–420.

Fodor, J., & Garrett, M. Some reflections on competence and performance. In J. Lyons & R. J. Wales (Eds.), *Psycholinguistic papers: The proceedings of the 1966 Edinburgh conference*. Edinburgh: Edinburgh University Press, 1966.

Franks, J. J., & Bransford, J. D. Abstraction of visual patterns. *Journal of Experimental Psychology*, 1971, **90**, 65–74.

Franks, J, J., & Bransford, J. D. The acquisition of abstract ideas. *Journal of Verbal Learning and Verbal Behavior,* 1972, **11**, 311–315.

Frase, L. T. Some data concerning the mathemagenic hypothesis. *American Educational Research Journal,* 1968, **5**, 181–189. (a)

Frase, L. T. Questions as aids to reading: Some research and theory. *American Educational Research Journal,* 1968, **5**, 319–322. (b)

Frase, L. T. Paragraph organization of written materials: The influence of conceptual clustering upon the level and organization of recall. *Journal of Educational Psychology,* 1969, **60**, 394–401.

Frase, L. T. Boundary conditions for mathemagenic behaviors. *Review of Educational Research,* 1970, **40**, 337–347.

Frase, L. T., & Silbiger, F. Some adaptive consequences of searching for information in a text. *American Educational Research Journal,* 1970, **7**, 553–560.

Fries, C. C. *Linguistics and reading.* New York: Holt, Rinehart & Winston, 1964.

Gardner, B. T., & Gardner, R. A. Two-way communication with an infant chimpanzee. In A. M. Schrier & F. Stollnitz (Eds.), *Behavior of non-human primates. Modern research trends,* vol. 4. New York: Academic, 1971.

Garrett, M., Bever, T., & Fodor, J. The active use of grammar in speech perception. *Perception and Psychophysiology,* 1966, **1**, 30–32.

Gleason, H. A., Jr. *An introduction to descriptive linguistics.* New York: Holt, Rinehart & Winston, 1960.

Gomez, A. What am I about? *Con Safos,* 1968, **1**, 8–9.

Goodman, K. S. Reading: A psycholinguistic guessing game. In H. Singer & R. B. Ruddell (Eds.), *Theoretical models and processes of reading.* Newark, Del.: International Reading Association, 1970.

Greenberg, J. H., & Jenkins, J. J. Studies in the psychological correlates of the sound system of American English. *Word,* 1964, **20**, 157–177.

Greeno, J. G. On the acquisition of a simple cognitive structure. In E. Tulving & W. Donaldson (Eds.), *Organization of memory.* New York: Academic Press, 1972.

Haugen, E. *Bilingualism in the Americas: A bibliography and research guide.* American Dialect Society, publication no. 26. University, Ala.: University of Alabama, 1956.

Hayes, W. D. My brother is a genius. In E. A. Betts & C. M. Welch (Eds.), *Adventures now and then,* 3rd ed., Book 6, Betts Basic Readers. New York: American Book, 1963.

Heidbreder, E. The attainment of concepts: I. Terminology and methodology. *Journal of General Psychology,* 1946, **35**, 173–189.

Huey, E. B. *The psychology and pedagogy of reading.* New York: Macmillan, 1908.

Hydén, H. Biochemical aspects of learning and memory. In K. Pribram (Ed.), *On the biology of learning.* New York: Harcourt Brace Jovanovich, 1969.

Jakobson, R. *Child language aphasia and phonological universals.* A. R. Keiler, Trans. The Hague: Mouton, 1968.

Jenkins, J. J., Foss, D. J., & Greenberg, J. H. Phonological distinctive features as cues in learning. *Journal of Experimental Psychology,* 1968, **77**, 200–205.

Jenkins, J. J., & Palermo, D. S. Mediation processes and the acquisition of linguistic structure. *Monographs of the Society for Research in Child Development,* 1964, **29**, 141–169.

John, V. P., & Horner, V. M. Bilingualism and the Spanish-speaking child. In F. Williams (Ed.), *Language and poverty: Perspectives on a theme.* Chicago: Markham, 1970.

Julesz, B. Cooperative phenomena in binocular depth perception. *American Scientist,* 1974, **62**, 32–43.

Katz, J. J. *The philosophy of language.* New York: Harper & Row, 1966.

Katz, J. J., & Fodor, J. A. The structure of a semantic theory. *Language,* 1963, **39**, 170–210.

Katz, J. J., & Postal, P. M. *An integrated theory of linguistic descriptions.* Cambridge: Massachusetts Institute of Technology Press, 1964.

Kohlberg, L., & Mayer, R. Development as the aim of education. *Harvard Educational Review,* 1972, **42**, 449–496.

Kuhn, T. S. *The structure of scientific revolutions,* 2nd ed. Chicago: University of Chicago Press, 1970.

Labov, W. *The study of non-standard English.* Washington, D. C.: Center for Applied Linguistics, 1969.

Lachman, R., & Dooling, D. J. Connected discourse and random strings: Effect of number of inputs on recognition and recall. *Journal of Experimental Psychology,* 1968, **77**, 517–522.

Ladefoged, P. The perception of speech. In *Mechanisation of thought process.* London: H. M. Stationery Office, 1959.

Lambert, W. E. A social psychology of bilingualism. *The Journal of Social Issues,* 1967, **23**(2), 91–109.

Lambert, W. E., & Jakobovits, L. A. Verbal satiation and changes in the intensity of meaning. *Journal of Experimental Psychology,* 1960, **60**, 376–383.

Lambert, W. E., & Macnamara, J. Some cognitive consequences of following a first-grade curriculum in a second language. *Journal of Educational Psychology,* 1969, **60**, 86–96.

Lenneberg, E. H. On explaining language. *Science,* 1969, **164**, 635–643.

Lewis, H. B. Studies in the principles of judgments and attitudes: IV. The operation of "prestige suggestion." *Journal of Social Psychology,* 1941, **14**, 229–256.

Lindsay, P. H., & Norman, D. A. *Human information processing. An introduction to psychology.* New York: Academic, 1972.

Lorge, I. Prestige, suggestion, and attitudes. *Journal of Social Psychology,* 1936, **7**, 386–402.

Luria, A. R. *The role of speech in the regulation of normal and abnormal behavior,* J. Tizard, Ed. Oxford: Pergamon, 1961.

Macnamara, J. The bilingual's linguistic performance—A psychological overview. *Journal of Social Issues,* 1967, **23**, 58–77.

Martin, C. J., Boersma, F. J., & Cox, D. L. A classification of associative strategies in paired-associate learning. *Psychonomic Science,* 1965, **3**, 455–456.

McAllister, D. E. The effects of various kinds of relevant verbal pre-training on subsequent motor performance. *Journal of Experimental Psychology,* 1953, **46**, 329–336.

McNeill, D. Developmental psycholinguistics. In F. Smith & G. A. Miller (Eds.), *The genesis of language: A psycholinguistic approach.* Cambridge: Massachusetts Institute of Technology Press, 1966.

McNeill, D. *The acquisition of language: The study of developmental psycholinguistics.* New York: Harper & Row, 1970.

McNeill, D. The capacity for the ontogenesis of grammar. In D. I. Slobin (Ed.), *The ontogenesis of grammar: A theoretical symposium.* New York: Academic Press, 1971.

Mednick, S. A., & Mednick, M. T. *Remote associates test.* Boston: Houghton Mifflin, 1967.

Menyuk, P. *The acquisition and development of language.* Englewood Cliffs, N. J.: Prentice-Hall, 1971.

Messer, S. Implicit phonology in children. *Journal of Verbal Learning and Verbal Behavior*, 1967, **6**, 609–613.

Miller, C. F., & Cofer, C. N. Cued recall from a categorized word list in Brazil in 1928. *Journal of Verbal Learning and Verbal Behavior*, 1972, **11**, 809–811.

Miller, G. A. Some psychological studies of grammar. *American Psychologist*, 1962, **17**, 748–762.

Miller, G. A., Galanter, E., & Pribram, K. H. *Plans and the structure of behavior.* New York: Holt, 1960.

Miller, W., & Ervin, S. M. The development of grammar in child language. In U. Bellugi & R. Brown (Eds.), The acquisition of language. *Monograph of the Society for Research in Child Development*, 1964, **29**(1), 9–34.

Miron, M. S., & Osgood, C. E. The multivariate structure of qualification. In R. B. Cattell (Ed.), *Handbook of multivariate experimental psychology.* Chicago: Rand McNally, 1966.

Olson, D. R. Language and thought: Aspects of a cognitive theory of semantics. *Psychological Review*, 1970, **77**, 257–273. (a)

Olson, D. R. *Cognitive development: The child's acquisition of diagonality.* New York: Academic, 1970. (b)

Osgood, C. E. The cross-cultural generality of visual-verbal synesthetic tendencies. *Behavioral Science*, 1960, **5**, 146–169.

Osgood, C. E., Suci, G. J., & Tannenbaum, P. H. *The measurement of meaning.* Urbana: University of Illinois Press, 1957.

Paivio, A. Imagery and language. In S. J. Segal (Ed.), *Imagery: Current cognitive approaches.* New York: Academic Press, 1971.

Palermo, D. S. More about less: A study of language comprehension. *Journal of Verbal Learning and Verbal Behavior*, 1973, **12**, 211–221.

Pavlov, I. P. *Conditioned reflexes: An investigation of the physiological activity of the cerebral cortex*, G. V. Anrye, Trans. and Ed. London: Oxford University Press, 1927.

Peal, E., & Lambert, W. E. The relation of bilingualism to intelligence. *Psychological Monographs*, 1962, **76**, whole no. 546.

Peterson, L. R., & Peterson, M. J. Short-term retention of individual verbal items. *Journal of Experimental Psychology*, 1959, **58**, 193–198.

Piaget, J. Development and learning. In R. E. Ripple & V. N. Rockcastle (Eds.), *Piaget rediscovered: A report of the conference on cognitive studies and curriculum development.* Ithaca, N. Y.: Cornell University, 1964.

Piaget, J., & Inhelder, B. *The psychology of the child,* H. Weaver, Trans. New York: Basic Books, 1969.

Polanyi, M. *The tacit dimension.* Garden City, N. Y.: Doubleday, 1966.

Pompi, K. F., & Lachman, R. Surrogate processes in the short-term retention of connected discourse. *Journal of Experimental Psychology*, 1967, **75**, 143–150.

Posner, M. I. Abstraction and the process of recognition. In G. H. Bower & J. T. Spence (Eds.), *The psychology of learning and motivation.* New York: Academic Press, 1969.

Premack, D. On the assessment of language competence in the chimpanzee. In A. M. Schrier & F. Stollnitz (Eds.), *Behavior of non-human primates. Modern research trends*, vol. 4. New York: Academic, 1971.

Quillian, M. R. Semantic memory. In M. Minsky (Ed.), *Semantic information processing*. Cambridge: Massachusetts Institute of Technology Press, 1968.

Robinson, F. G. *Study guide for Ausubel/Robinson school learning: An introduction to educational psychology*. New York: Holt, Rinehart & Winston, 1970.

Rohrman, N. L. The role of syntactic structure in the recall of English nominalizations. *Journal of Verbal Learning and Verbal Behavior*, 1968, **7**, 904–912.

Rosenbaum, P. S. *The grammar of English predicate complement constructions*. Research Monograph No. 47. Cambridge: Massachusetts Institute of Technology Press, 1967.

Rothkopf, E. Z. Learning from written instructive material: An exploration of the control of inspection behavior by test-like events. *American Educational Research Journal*, 1966, **3**, 241–249.

Rothkopf, E. Z. The concept of mathemagenic activities. *Review of Educational Research*, 1970, **40**, 325–336.

Rothkopf, E. Z., & Bisbicos, E. E. Selective facilitative effects of interspersed questions on learning from written materials. *Journal of Educational Psychology*, 1967, **58**, 56–61.

Rothkopf, E. Z., & Coke, E. U. Variations in phrasing, repetition intervals, and the recall of sentence material. *Journal of Verbal Learning and Verbal Behavior*, 1966, **5**, 86–91.

Rubenstein, H., Garfield, L., & Millikan, J. Homographic entries in the internal lexicon. *Journal of Verbal Learning and Verbal Behavior*, 1970, **9**, 487–494.

Saltz, E. *The cognitive bases of human learning*. Homewood, Ill.: Dorsey Press, 1971.

Savin, H. B., & Bever, T. G. The non-perceptual reality of the phoneme. *Journal of Verbal Learning and Verbal Behavior*, 1970, **9**, 295–302.

Schultz, C. B., & Di Vesta, F. J. The effects of passage organization and note-taking on the selection of clustering strategies and on recall of textual material. *Journal of Educational Psychology*, 1972, **63**, 244–252.

Seibel, R. *Organization in human verbal learning*. Paper presented at the meeting of the Psychonomic Society, Chicago, October, 1965.

Seibel, R. *Organization in human learning: Some more on the study sheet paradigm and an experiment with "exhaustive" categories*. Paper presented at the meeting of the Psychonomic Society, St. Louis, October, 1966.

Shavelson, R. J. Methods for examining representations of a science subject-matter structure in a student's memory. *Journal of Research in Science Teaching*, 1973, in press.

Sherif, M. A study of some social factors in perception. *Archives of Psychology*, 1935, no. 187.

Skinner, B. F. *Verbal behavior*. New York: Appleton-Century-Crofts, 1957.

Slobin, D. I. The acquisition of Russian as a native language. In F. Smith & G. A. Miller (Eds.), *The genesis of language: A psycholinguistic approach*. Cambridge: Massachusetts Institute of Technology Press, 1966.

Smith, F. *Understanding reading—A psycholinguistic analysis of reading and learning to read*. New York: Holt, Rinehart & Winston, 1971.

Smith, M. E. An investigation of the development of the sentence and the extent of the vocabulary in young children. *University of Iowa Studies of Child Welfare*, 1926, **3**(5), serial no. 109.

Snider, J. G., & Osgood, C. E., Eds. *Semantic differential techniques*. Chicago: Aldine, 1969.

Spiker, C. C. Experiments with children on the hypothesis of acquired distinctiveness and equivalence of cues. *Child Development*, 1956, **27**, 253–263.

158   References

Stewart, W. A. On the use of Negro dialect in the teaching of reading. In J. C. Baratz & R. W. Shuy (Eds.), *Teaching black children to read.* Washington, D. C.: Center for Applied Linguistics, 1969.

Taylor, W. L. "Cloze procedure": A new tool for measuring readability. *Journalism Quarterly*, 1953, **30**, 415–433.

Templin, M. C. *Certain language skills in children: Their development and interrelationships.* Institute for Child Welfare Monograph Series, No. 26. Minneapolis: University of Minnesota Press, 1957.

Tulving, E. Episodic and semantic memory. In E. Tulving & W. Donaldson (Eds.), *Organization of memory.* New York: Academic Press, 1972.

Tulving, E., & Pearlstone, Z. Availability versus accessibility of information in memory for words. *Journal of Verbal Learning and Verbal Behavior*, 1966, **5**, 381–391.

Valentine, C. A. Deficit, difference, and bicultural models of Afro-American behavior. *Harvard Educational Review*, 1971, **41**, 137–157.

Vygotsky, L. S. *Thought and language.* E. Hanfmann & G. Vakar, Trans. and Eds. Cambridge: Massachusetts Institute of Technology Press, 1962.

Werner, H., & Kaplan, E. Development of word meaning through verbal context: An experimental study. *Journal of Psychology*, 1950, **29**, 251–257.

Whorf, B. L. Science and linguistics. In J. B. Carroll (Ed.), *Language, thought, and reality.* Cambridge, Mass.: The Technology Press and John Wiley, 1956.

Wickelgren, W. A. Context-sensitive coding, associative memory, and serial order in (speech) behavior. *Psychological Review*, 1969, **76**, 1–15.

Wolfram, W. Social dialects from a linguistic perspective. In R. W. Shuy (Ed.), *Sociolinguistics: A cross-disciplinary approach.* Washington, D. C.: Center for Applied Linguistics, 1971.

Yavuz, H. S., & Bousfield, W. A. Recall of connotative meaning. *Psychological Reports*, 1959, **5**, 319–320.

Yeni-Komshian, G. H., & Lambert, W. E. Concurrent and consecutive modes of learning two vocabularies. *Journal of Educational Psychology*, 1969, **60**, 204–215.

AUTHOR INDEX

SUBJECT INDEX

CAMROSE LUTHERAN COLLEGE LIBRARY